Helen Kendrick Johnson

**Woman and the Republic**

A Survey of the Woman-Suffrage Movement in the United States

Helen Kendrick Johnson

**Woman and the Republic**
*A Survey of the Woman-Suffrage Movement in the United States*

ISBN/EAN: 9783337062460

Printed in Europe, USA, Canada, Australia, Japan

Cover: Foto ©ninafisch / pixelio.de

More available books at **www.hansebooks.com**

# WOMAN AND THE REPUBLIC

A SURVEY OF THE WOMAN-SUFFRAGE
MOVEMENT IN THE UNITED STATES
AND A DISCUSSION OF THE CLAIMS
AND ARGUMENTS OF ITS FOREMOST
ADVOCATES : : : : : : : : : BY
HELEN KENDRICK JOHNSON

NEW YORK
D. APPLETON AND COMPANY
M DCCC XCVII

# CONTENTS.

### CHAPTER I.
PAGE

INTRODUCTORY.................................... 5

### CHAPTER II.
IS WOMAN SUFFRAGE DEMOCRATIC?.................. 10

### CHAPTER III.
WOMAN SUFFRAGE AND THE AMERICAN REPUBLIC...... 39

### CHAPTER IV.
WOMAN SUFFRAGE AND PHILANTHROPY................ 106

### CHAPTER V.
WOMAN SUFFRAGE AND THE LAWS................... 156

### CHAPTER VI.
WOMAN SUFFRAGE AND THE TRADES ................ 186

### CHAPTER VII.
WOMAN SUFFRAGE AND THE PROFESSIONS........ .... 210

### CHAPTER VIII.
WOMAN SUFFRAGE AND EDUCATION................... 222

### CHAPTER IX.
WOMAN SUFFRAGE AND THE CHURCH........ ......... 246

4 *CONTENTS.*

## CHAPTER X.

PAGE

WOMAN SUFFRAGE AND SEX.......................... 278

## CHAPTER XI.

WOMAN SUFFRAGE AND THE HOME ................... 302

## CHAPTER XII.

CONCLUSION... ..................................... 320

# WOMAN AND THE REPUBLIC.

## CHAPTER I.

THE introduction to the "History of Woman Suffrage," published in 1881–85, edited by Elizabeth Cady Stanton, Susan B. Anthony and Matilda Joslyn Gage, contains the following statement : "It is often asserted that, as woman has ' always been man's slave, subject, inferior, dependent, under all forms of government and religion, slavery must be her normal condition ; but that her condition is abnormal is proved by the marvellous change in her character, from a toy in the Turkish harem, or a drudge in the Geramn fields, to a leader of thought in the literary circles of France, England, and America."

I have made this quotation partly on account of its direct application to the subject to be discussed, and partly to illustrate the contradictions that seem to inhere in the arguments on which the claim to Woman Suffrage is founded. If woman has become a leader of thought in the literary circles of the most cultivated lands, she

5

has not always been man's slave, subject, inferior, dependent, under all forms of government and religion; and, furthermore, it is not true that there has been such a marvellous change in her character as is implied in this statement. Where man is a bigot and a barbarian, there, alas! woman is still a harem toy; where man is little more than a human clod, woman is to-day a drudge in the field; where man has hewn the way to governmental and religious freedom, there woman has become a leader of thought. The unity of race progress is strikingly suggested by this fact. The method through which that unity is maintained should unfold itself as we study the story of the sex advancement of our time.

Progress is a magic word, and the Suffrage party has been fortunate in its attempt to invoke the sorcery of the thought that it enfolds, and to blend it with the claim of woman to share in the public duty of voting. Possession of the elective franchise is a symbol of power in man's hand; why should it not bear the same relation to woman's upward impulse and action? Modern adherents ask, " Is not the next new force at hand in our social evolution to come from the entrance of woman upon the political arena ? " The roots of these questions, and consequently of their answers, lie as deep as the roots of being, and they cannot be laid bare by superficial digging. But the laying bare of roots is not the only way, or even the best way, to judge of the strength and beauty of a growth. We look at the leaves, the flowers, and the fruit. "Movement" and "Progress" are not synonymous terms. In evolution there is degeneration as well as regeneration. Only the work that has been in accord with the highest ideals of woman's nature is fitted to the environment of its advance, and thus to survival and development. In order to learn whether Woman Suffrage is in the line of advance, we must know whether the movement to obtain it has thus far blended itself with those that have proved to be for woman's progress and for the progress of government.

I am sure I need not emphasize the fact that, in studying some of the principles that underlie the Suffrage movement, I am not impugning the motives of the leaders. Nor need I dwell upon the fact that it is from the good comradeship of men and women that has come to prevail under our free conditions, that some women have hastily espoused a cause with which they never have affiliated, because they supposed it to be fighting against odds for the freedom of their sex.

The past fifty years have wrought more change in the conditions of life than could many a Cathayan cycle. The growth of religious liberty, enlargement of foreign and home missions, the Temperance movement, the giant war waged for principle, are among the causes of this change. The settlement of the great West, the opening of professions and trades to woman consequent upon the loss of more than a half million of the nation's most stalwart men, the mechanical inventions that have changed home and trade conditions, the sudden advance of science, the expansion of mind and of work that are fostered by the play of a free government,—all these have tended to place man and woman, but especially woman, where something like a new heaven and a new earth are in the distant vision.

To this change the Suffragists call attention, and say, " This is, in great part, our work." In this little book I shall recount a few of the facts that, in my opinion, go to prove that the Suffrage movement has had but little part or lot in this matter. And because of these facts I believe the principles on which the claim to suffrage is founded are those that turn individuals and nations backward and not forward.

The first proof I shall mention is the latest one in time—it is the fact of an Anti-Suffrage movement. In the political field alone are we being formed into separate camps whose watch-words become more unlike as they become more clearly understood. The fact that for the first time in our history representatives of two great organizations of women are appealing to courts and legislatures, each begging them to refuse the prayer of the other, shows, as conclu-sively as a long argument could do, that this matter of suffrage is something essentially dis-tinct from the great series of movements in which women thus far have advanced side by side. It is an instinctive announcement of a belief that the demand for suffrage is not progress; that it does array sex against sex; that woman, like man, can advance only as the race advances; and that here lies the dividing line.

How absolute is that dividing line between woman's progress and woman suffrage, we may realize when we consider what the result would be if we could know to-morrow, beyond a peradventure, that woman never would vote in the United States. Not one of her charities, great or small, would be crippled. Not a woman's college would close its doors. Not a profession would withhold its diploma from her; not a trade its recompense. Not a single just law would be repealed, or a bad one framed, as a consequence. Not a good book would be forfeited. Not a family would be less secure of domestic happiness. Not a single hope would die which points to a time when our cities will all be like those of the prophet's vision, "first pure and then peaceable."

Among the forces that are universally considered progressive are : the democratic idea in government, extinction of slavery, increase of educational and industrial opportunities for woman, improvement in the statute laws, and spread of religious freedom. The Woman-Suffrage movement professed to champion these causes. That movement is now nearly fifty years old, and has made a record by which its relation to them can be judged. What is the verdict?

# CHAPTER II.

As the claim of woman to share the voting power is related to the fundamental principles of government, the progress of government must be studied in relation to that claim in order to learn its bearing upon them. It is possible to suggest in one brief chapter only the barest outline of such a far-reaching scrutiny, and wiser heads than mine must search to conclusion ; but some beginnings looking toward an answer to the inquiry I have raised have occurred to me as not having entered into the newly-opened controversy on woman suffrage.

I say, the newly-opened controversy, for, through these fifty years, the Suffragists have done nearly all the talking. So persistently have they laid claim to being in the line of progress for woman, that many of their newly aroused opponents fancied that the anti-suffrage view might be the ultra conservative one, and that democratic principles, strictly and broadly applied, might at last lead to woman suffrage, though premature if pushed to a conclusion now.

10

The first step in finding out how far that position is true is, to ascertain what the Suffragists say about this noblest of democracies, our own Government. In referring to the "The History of Woman Suffrage" for the opinions of the leaders, I am not only using a book that on its publication was considered a strong and full presentment of their arguments, but one which they are to-day advertising and selling as "a perfect arsenal of the work done by and for women during the last half century." In it the editors say: "Woman's political equality with man is the legitimate outgrowth of the fundamental principles . of our government." Dr. Mary Putnam Jacobi, writing in the New York Sun in April, 1894, says : " Never, until the establishment of universal [male] suffrage, did it happen that all the women in a community, no matter how well born, how intelligent, how well educated, how virtuous, how wealthy, were counted the political inferiors of all the men, no matter how base born, how stupid, how ignorant, how brutal, how poverty-stricken. This anomaly is the real innovation. Men have personally ruled the women of their families; the law has annihilated the separate existence of women; but women have never been subjected to the political sovereignty of all men simply in virtue of their sex. Never, that is, since the days of the ancient republics." Mrs. Ellen Battelle Dietrick, who, as Secretary of the New-England Suffrage Association, was put forward to meet all comers, writing in July, 1895, said: "Shall we, as a people, be true to our principles and enfranchise woman? or, shall we drift along in the meanest form of oligarchy known among men— an oligarchy which exalts every sort of a male into a ruler simply because he is a male, and debases every woman into a subject simply because she is a woman?" Mrs. Fanny B. Ames, speaking in Boston in 1896, said: "I believe woman suffrage to be the final result of the evolution of a true democracy." Not only has every woman speaker or writer in favor of suffrage presented this idea in some form, but the men also who have taken that side have done likewise. One among those who advocated the cause before the Committee in the Constitutional Convention of New York, said: "Woman Suffrage is the inevitable result of the logic of the situation of modern society. The despot who first yielded an inch of power gave up the field. We are standing in the light of the best interests of the State of New York when we stand in the way of this forward movement."

All these writers charge the American Republic with being false to democratic principles in excluding women from the franchise, while but one of them alludes to the fact that in the ancient republics the same "anomaly" was seen.

As I read political history, the facts go to show that the fundamental principles of our Government are more opposed to the exercise of suffrage

by women than are those of monarchies.  To me it
seems that both despotism and anarchy are more
friendly to woman's political aspirations than is
any form of constitutional government, and that
manhood suffrage, and not womanhood suffrage,
is the final result of the evolution of democracy.

The Suffragists repeatedly call attention to the
fact that in the early ages in Egypt, in Greece,
and in Rome, women were of much greater political consequence than later during the republics;
but the moral they have drawn has been that of
the superiority of the ancient times.  Mrs. Dietrick says: "The ideal woman of Greece was
Athena, patroness of all household arts and indus-
tries, but equally patroness of all political interests.  The greatest city of Greece was believed to
have been founded by her, and Greek history
recorded that, though the men citizens voted
solidly to have the city named for Neptune, yet
the women citizens voted solidly for Athena, beat
them by one vote, and carried that political matter.  If physical force had been a governing
power in Greece, and men its manifestation, how
could such a story have been published by Greek
men down to the second century before our era?"

Mrs. Dietrick's remarkably realistic version of
the old myth does not tell the tale as Greek men
published it.  Varro, who was educated at Athens, goes on to say: "Thereupon, Neptune became enraged, and immediately the sea flowed
over all the land of Athens.  To appease the god,

the burgesses were compelled to impose a three-fold punishment upon their wives—they were to lose their votes; the children were to receive no more the mother's name; and they themselves were no longer to be called Athenians, after the goddess." It seems to me this fable teaches that physical force was indeed the governing power in Athens at that day, and that men were its manifestation.

The legend is generally taken to indicate the time when the Greek gens progressed to the family. In the ruder time, the legitimacy of the chieftain might be traced, because the mother, though not always the father, could be known with certainty. When the father became the acknowledged head of the household, a distinct advance was made toward that heroic age in which the vague but towering figures of men and women move across the stage. Goddesses, queens, princesses, are powerful in love and war. Sibyls unfold the meaning of the book of fate. Vestals feed the fires upon the highest and lowest altars. Later, throughout most of the states of Greece, something like the following order of political life is seen: from kings to oligarchs, from oligarchs to tyrants or despots, from them to some form of restricted constitutional liberty. In Sparta, all change of government was controlled by the machinery of war, and the soldiers were made forever free. Athens, separated from the rest of Greece, was less agitated by outward conflict. In government she passed from king to archon; from hereditary archon to archons chosen for ten years, but always from one family, then to those elected for one year, nine being chosen. At the time of the Areopagus there were four classes of citizens. The first three paid taxes, had a right to share in the government, and formed the defence of the state. If women were of political importance in earlier times, and if a republic is more favorable to the exercise by them of the elective franchise, we should expect to find women reaching their highest power under the Areopagus. Exactly the contrary appears to be true. Native and honorable Greek women retired to domestic life as the liberty of their people grew. Grote, in his " History of Greece," referring to the legendary period, says : " We find the wife occupying a station of great dignity and influence, though it was the practice of the husband to purchase her by valuable presents to her parents. She even seems to live less secluded, and to enjoy a wider sphere of action, than was allotted to her in historic Greece."

Lecky, in his " European Morals," says : " It is one of the most remarkable and, to some writers, one of the most perplexing facts in the moral history of Greece, that in the former and ruder period women had undoubtedly the highest place, and their type exhibited the highest perfection." What the " highest perfection " is, for her type, or for man's type, is not here under discussion ;

but it is not out of place to say in passing that if the final conquest of the spiritual over the material forces of humanity is really the aim of civilization, these " facts in the moral history of Greece " become less " perplexing."

The heroines of Homer's tales were all of noble birth—they were goddesses, princesses, hereditary gentlewomen. In early historic times, also, it was only royal or gentle blood that secured for woman political power. Athena was, in gentle Athens, patroness of household arts ; but in Sparta, as Minerva, the same divinity was goddess, not of political interests, as Mrs. Dietrick puts it, but of war. She sprang full-armed from the head of Jove—rather a masculine origin, it must be owned. In Sparta women became soldiers as the democratic idea advanced. Princess Archidamia, marching at the head of her female troop to rebuke the senators for the decree that the women and children be removed from the city before the anticipated attack could come, is an example. In Etolia, in Argos, and in other states, the same was true. Maria and Telesilla led the women in battle and disciplined them in peace. But the world does not turn to Sparta for its ideal of a pre-Christian republic, and the Suffragists of our day do not propose to emulate the Spartan Amazon and hew their way to political power with the sword.

In Athens, which does present the model, matters were far otherwise. In the year 700 B. C., the Spartans called upon Athens for a commander to lead them to the second Messenian war, and the Athenians sent them Tyrtæus, their martial poet. The Spartans were displeased at his youth and gentle bearing; but when the battle was joined, his chanting of his own warsongs so animated the troops that they won against heavy odds. The following is a fragment translated from one of his lyrics:

" But be it ours to guard the hallowed spot,
    To shield the tender offspring and the wife;
Here steadily await our destined lot,
    And, for their sakes, resign the gift of life."

Æschylus, poet and soldier, writing a hundred and fifty years later, in his "Seven Against Thebes," puts into the mouth of the chieftain Eteocles this address to the women:

" It is not to be borne, ye wayward race;
Is this your best, is this the aid you lend
The state, the fortitude with which you steel
The souls of the besieged, thus falling down
Before the images to wail, and shriek
With lamentations loud ?  Wisdom abhors you.
Nor in misfortune, nor in dear success,
Be woman my associate.  If her power
Bears sway, her insolence exceeds all bounds;
But if she fears, woe to that house and city.
And now by holding counsel with weak fear,
You magnify the foe, and turn our men
To flight.  Thus are we ruined by ourselves.
This ever will arise from suffering women
To intermix with men.  But mark me well,
Whoe'er henceforth dares disobey my orders—

2

Be it man or woman, old or young—
Vengeance shall burst upon him, the decree
Stands irreversible, and he shall die.
War is no female province, but the scene
For men. Hence, home! nor spread your mischiefs here.
Hear you, or not? Or speak I to the deaf?"

Pericles, in his famous funeral oration over those who fell in the Peloponnesian war, thus addresses the Athenian women : "To the wives who will henceforth live in widowhood, I will speak, in one short sentence only, of womanly virtue. She is the best woman who is most truly a woman, and her reputation is the highest whose name is never in the mouths of men for good or for evil."

Seclusion was the best thing that the most intellectual pre-Christian republic could give to its honorable women. The freedom with which the hetairæ, who were foreigners or daughters of slaves, mingled with statesmen and philosophers, brought them open political influence, but not a hint of voting power or of office-holding.

For the sake of brevity, I will confine my reference to Roman custom to a single pregnant sentence from Gibbon's "Decline and Fall of the Empire." He says : "In every age and country the wiser, or at least the stronger of the two sexes, has usurped the powers of the state, and confined the other to the cares and pleasures of domestic life. In hereditary monarchies, however, and especially in those of modern Europe, the gallant

spirit of chivalry, and the law of succession, have
accustomed us to allow a singular exception, and
a woman is often acknowledged the absolute
sovereign of a great kingdom, in which she would
be deemed incapable of exercising the smallest
employment, civil or military.  But, as the Roman
Emperors were still considered as the generals
and magistrates of the Republic, their wives and
mothers, although dignified by the name of
Augusta, were never associated to their personal
honors; and a female reign would have appeared
an inexplicable prodigy in the eyes of those primitive Romans, who married without love, or loved
without delicacy or respect."

The warlike states named republics in the
Middle Ages had no woman Doge, or Duke, although women rose to the semblance of political
power with empires and kingdoms, in Italy and
Spain as well as in Germany and France, Austria
and Russia.

Let us turn to modern Europe, in which thrones
have been occupied now and again by queens.
The progress of woman here, especially in Anglo-
Saxon countries, has been steady, true and inspiring.  In the earliest recorded councils of the
race from which we sprang, we see freemen in
full armor casting equal votes.  During the ages
of feudalism, women who were land-owners had
the same rights as other nobles.  They could
raise soldiery, coin money, and administer justice
in both civil and criminal proceedings.  In pro-

portion as the aristocratic power lost its hold,
women were exempted from these services and
gained in moral influence. The Germanic races
were renowned for their respect for woman, and
their love for home. As constitutional liberty
grew, and each Englishman's house became his
castle for defence against arbitrary power, the
protection was not for himself but for his family.
A figure-head ruler in feminine attire sits on
England's throne to-day—the England that still
unites its church and state, and in which feudal
customs still prevail to some extent. Widows
and spinsters who are property-owners can vote
for all offices except the one charged under the
Constitution with the framing and execution of
the laws of the land. Aristocracy decrees that
in the House of Lords the Bishops shall have a
voice; but in the House of Commons no clergyman can hold a seat, and for members of Parliament no woman votes. Would any Suffragist
hold that a clergyman was the inferior of men
who do sit in the House of Commons? They
are excluded for the same reason that woman has
not the parliamentary vote—they are looked upon
as non-combatants.

The Greek and Roman republics appear to have
followed an instinct that was unerring in the
condition of society when they removed women
from the seats of power as the commonwealth
gathered strength. Gibbon, in the sentences
quoted, attributes the fact that queens as well as

kings have occupied the thrones of modern Europe to the chivalry of men toward those who would yet be incapable of exercising actual power except for the backing of a standing army, or an hereditary nobility sworn to their support, both of which are composed solely of men. If this be true, it should be visible in the workings of the constitutional restrictions upon monarchies that have developed in the past fifty years, during which the principle of democratic government has advanced with enormous strides over a great portion of the globe.

In the Austro-Hungarian monarchy there is restricted woman suffrage. The kingdom of Italy has restricted municipal woman suffrage. The little republic that separates those countries, the land of Tell and the Vaudois, has direct manhood suffrage only.

Sweden and Norway are apparently parting company. Sweden chooses to keep its king and its aristocracy, and it has restricted woman suffrage; but Norway, which is working toward free institutions, and last year voted to remove the insignia of union from the Norwegian flag, has no woman suffrage.*

* In the city of Berne, Switzerland, in 1852, a proxy vote was given to independent women who paid a commercial tax, but they made no effort to use it until 1885, when contending political factions compelled them to do so in a measure. Norway's women have a local school vote. Both these cases of exception serve to prove the rule that I am trying to set forth.

Autocratic Russia and its Asiatic colonies have more woman suffrage than England. Finland, a constitutional monarchy, was ceded to the Emperor of Russia in 1809. Women there have all except the parliamentary suffrage. The Governor-General of the Senate is nominated by the Emperor, and is chief of the military force. The National Assembly is convoked by the Emperor whenever he sees fit. The duties of that Assembly are to consider laws proposed by the Emperor and elaborated by the Committee of Affairs and four members nominated by the Emperor, who sit in St. Petersburg. The Emperor has the veto power over any act of theirs. That National Assembly consists of representatives of the nobility, the clergy, the burghers, and the peasantry, the consent of all of whom must be obtained to any measure that makes a change in the constitution or imposes taxes. But the royal veto can set aside any decision.

Iceland, a dependency of Denmark, has municipal woman suffrage, and women are eligible to municipal office. It has its own legislature, which governs jointly with the King, the executive power being in the hands of the King alone.

In the great extensions of suffrage in England in 1848, an amendment for the extension of suffrage to women was introduced in Parliament by Mr. Disraeli. Lord Northcote, Lord John Manners, and other conservatives, upheld it; but the liberal leaders opposed it, Gladstone and John

Bright among them. John Bright's family were strenuous for the movement, and he had fancied himself its friend until the issue came; then the old champion of freedom proved true to the instinct that guards it in the nation. In the constantly increasing liberty of the lower classes of England, an essential principle which excludes women from the parliamentary vote has been maintained. Lady Spencer Churchill and other Suffrage leaders look to Viscount Templeton and Lord Salisbury for support to-day.

A woman-suffrage bill of many years' standing and absurd provisions, has just passed to a second reading in the House of Commons. Although it was treated as a joke by all parties, it served to emphasize the fact that Sir Vernon Harcourt and the Liberals are opposed to any advance in this direction.

In the late extension of suffrage in Canada, the movement for woman suffrage had conservative support, while every liberal leader opposed it. No South American Republic has woman suffrage. With the deposition of Liliuokalani, woman's direct political power in the Hawaiian Islands died. In France only the Anarchists "admit women" to public council, and that party in Germany has here and there inscribed woman suffrage upon its banners.

Not only England, Scotland and Wales, but Canada, definitely excepts the vote for members of parliament in giving suffrage to woman, and

only widows and spinsters are admitted to the
minor forms of franchise.   As to the other British
colonies, what is the situation ?   Much stress has
been laid on what has been termed the progress
of   the   Suffrage   movement   in   Australasia.
There is but one Australian colony in which the
legislative assembly is elected ; in the others it is
appointed for life, or for short terms.   Where it
is thus appointed, women vote on various matters.
In Victoria, which contains the capital city, Mel-
bourne, and which is the most progressive and
democratic colony in Australia, the Legislative
Assembly is elected, and that body is chosen by
unrestricted male suffrage only, while, as with
the House of Commons in the mother country,
clergymen are not allowed to sit in it.   In West
Australia, the newest colony, the voting is done
by men alone.   In Cape Colony women have restricted municipal suffrage ; but the Assembly is
elected by the vote of men who own a certain
amount of property.

In the Orange Free State every adult white
male is a full burgher, having a vote for the President, who is chosen for five years.   The Transvaal Republic has no woman suffrage amid its
hand-to-hand struggles.

To comprehend the condition of European governmental affairs, one must follow the condition
of things produced by the struggle of socialistic
and anarchistic elements.   Between the King on
the one hand, and these forces on the other, the

true Liberal parties are slowly progressing toward free institutions ; both aristocratic and anarchistic movements being more favorable than liberalism to woman-suffrage aspirations.

The countries where woman has full suffrage (save in the United States) are all dependencies of royalty. They are : The Isle of Man, Pitcairn's Island, New Zealand, and South Australia. The most important of these, New Zealand, was once a promising colony, but it has been declining for a quarter of a century. The men outnumber the women by forty thousand. The act conferring the parliamentary franchise on both European and Maori women received the royal sanction in 1892. At the session of Parliament that passed the act a tax was put upon incomes and one upon land, so that a desperate civilization seemed to be trying all the experiments at once. Certainly, woman suffrage in New Zealand was not adopted because the Government was so stable, so strong, so democratic, that these conditions must thus find fit expression.*

South Australia not only gives women full suffrage, but makes them eligible to a seat in Parliament. The colony is a vast, mountainous, largely unsettled region, with a high proportion of native

---

* The Australasian colonies are taking steps toward the formation of a Federal Union. While this book is in press news comes that the Federal Convention, by a vote of 23 to 12, has refused to allow women to vote for members of the House of Representatives.

and Chinese, and, in 1894, had but 73,000 voters, including the women. The Socialistic Labor movement, which has played a large part in Australasian politics, here succeeded in dominating the government. There was an attempt to establish communistic villages with public money, a proposal to divide the public money *pro rata*, and one to build up a system of state life-insurance ; and taxes were to be levied on salaries, and on all incomes above a certain point. It was found that the sixty thousand women who were authorized to vote throughout Australia assisted the socialistic schemes that are hindering progress and that tend to anarchy and not to republicanism. There is a royal Governor, and suffrage is based on household and property qualifications. It is an aristocratic and social combination, not a triumph of democratic ideas or principles. Dr. Jacobi, in her " Common Sense applied to Woman Suffrage," says : " The refusal to extend parliamentary suffrage to women who are possessed of municipal suffrage, does not mean, as Americans are apt to suppose, that women are counted able to judge about the small concerns of a town, but not about imperial issues. It means that women are still not counted able to exercise independent judgment at all, and, therefore, are to remain counted out when this is called for ; but that the property to which they happen to belong, and which requires representation, must not be deprived of this on account of an entangling female alliance. This is the very antipodes of the democratic doctrine, perhaps also somewhat excessive, that a man requires representation so much that he must not be deprived of it on account of the accident of not being able to read or write!"

With Dr. Jacobi's interpretation, I will deal later. What I wish now to do is, to call attention to her admission of the fact that woman suffrage in England and in her colonies is not democratic, and to connect it with the other fact that no republic, from that of Greece to our own, has introduced it, although manhood suffrage has been universal in Switzerland for many years, and in France since 1848.

So it would seem that under a monarchical system, with a standing army and a hereditary nobility to support the throne, the royal mandate could be issued by a woman. Any Queen, as well as the one that Alice met in Wonderland, could say, " Off with his head!" But when freedom grew, and the democratic idea began to prevail, and each individual man became a king, and each home a castle, the law given by God and not by man came into exercise, and upon each man was laid the duty of defending liberty and those who were physically unfitted to defend themselves.

Let us turn now to our own country. Technically, at least, women possessed the suffrage in our first settlements. In New England, in the early days, when church-membership as the

basis of the franchise excluded three-fourths of
the male inhabitants from its exercise, women
could vote.  Under the old Provincial charters,
from 1691 to 1780, they could vote for all elective
offices.  From 1780 to 1785, under the Articles
of Confederation, they could vote for all elective
offices except the Governor, the Council, and the
Legislature.  The comment made upon this by
the Suffrage writers is, that " the fact that woman
exercised the right of suffrage amid so many
restrictions, is very significant of the belief in her
right to the ballot-box."  My comment is, that
the same lesson we have learned in Europe is
repeated here with wonderful emphasis.  Under
the transported aristocracy of churchly power in
the state, they shared the undemocratic rule.
When freedom broadened a little, and, under a
system that still acknowledged allegiance to the
British Crown, all property-holders or other " duly
qualified " colonists could vote, they still had the
voice that England grants to-day, the voice of an
estate.  When liberty took another step and a
league was formed of " firm friendship " in which
each Colony was to be independent and yet
banded for offensive and defensive aid, the women
were retired from the special vote on the result of
which lay the actual execution of the law.  But
this country was not yet a republic, or even a
nation.  Washington himself said that the state
of things under the Articles of Confederation
was hardly removed from anarchy.  In 1789 a

constitution was adopted, which made the American people a nation. Its preamble read: "We, the people of the United States, in order to form a more perfect union, establish justice, insure domestic tranquillity, provide for the common defence, promote· the general welfare, and secure the blessings of liberty to ourselves and our posterity, do ordain and establish this Constitution for the United States of America." Under this Constitution the last vestiges of churchly political rule, and of property-qualification for voting, have gradually disappeared. New Jersey was the last State to repeal her property-qualification laws. In 1709 she made "male freeholders" who held a certain amount of property the only voters. In 1790 her Constitution, through an error in wording, admitted "all inhabitants" with certain property to vote. This was in force until 1807, when an act was passed conferring the suffrage upon "free white male citizens twenty-one years of age worth fifty pounds proclamation money, clear estate," etc. From 1790 to 1807 a good many women, generally from the Society of Friends, took part in elections. After 1807 they attempted to do so, as owners of property. Finally, that qualification for the male voter was done away with, and with it the woman-suffrage agitation disappeared.

State after State, in carrying out the compact of the Federal Republic, had inserted the word "male" into the Constitutions that embodied the

American conception of a more vital and enduring freedom.

But there are now four States of the Union where women have full suffrage, a few where they have a measure of municipal suffrage, and many where they have the school suffrage. What bearing do these facts have upon my claim that woman suffrage is undemocratic?

The States where they have full suffrage are Utah, Wyoming, Colorado, and Idaho. How far was its introduction into these States the result of advanced legislation in accord with true republicanism? Utah Territory was the first spot in the country in which the measure gained a foothold, and that was not believed by its introducers to be a part of the United States. The Mormons who founded Salt Lake City supposed themselves to be settling on Mexican territory, outside the jurisdiction of American law. Woman suffrage was almost coincident with its beginnings, and it came as a legitimate part of the union of state and church, of communism, of polygamy. The dangers that especially threaten a republican form of government are anarchy, communism, and religious bigotry; and two of these found their fullest expression, in this country, in the Mormon creed and practice. Fealty to Mormonism was disloyalty to the United States Government. Thus, the introduction of woman suffrage within our borders was not only undemocratic, it was anti-democratic.

Woman suffrage was secured in Wyoming by means that bring dishonor upon democracy. Wyoming was organized as a Territory in 1868. Many of its native settlers were from Utah. For its vast, mountainous extent of nearly 98,000 square miles, the census gave a population of only 9,118 persons. Of these the native-born numbered 5,605, foreign-born, 3,513. The males numbered 7,219 ; the females, 1,899. The "History of Woman Suffrage" records the fact that the measure was secured in the first Territorial legislature through the political trickery of an illiterate and discredited man, who was in the chair. Mr. Bryce, in "The American Commonwealth," alludes in a note to the same fact. Women voted in 1870. In 1871 a bill was passed repealing the suffrage act, but was vetoed by the Governor, on the ground that, having been admitted, it must be given a fair trial. An attempt to pass the repeal over his veto was lost by a single vote. Certainly, the entrance of woman suffrage into Wyoming was not a triumph of democratic progress and principle.

Colorado was admitted into the Union in 1876, and great efforts were made by Suffragists to secure the "Centennial" State. This resulted in a submission of the question to the people, who rejected it by a majority of 7,443 in a total vote of 20,665. From the first of the agitation for the free coinage of silver, Colorado has been enthusiastically in favor of that measure. In 1892 her devotion to it caused all parties to unite on that issue and gave the vote of the State to General Weaver, Populist candidate for President, and to David H. Waite, Populist candidate for Governor. The question of woman suffrage was re-submitted to the people at this election, and the constitutional amendment concerning it was carried by a majority of only 5,000 in a total vote of 200,000. Neither that movement nor its results present triumphant democracy.

In 1894 the Populist party of Idaho put a plank in its platform favoring the submission of a woman-suffrage amendment to the people. In 1896 the Free Silver Populist movement swept the State. A majority of the votes cast on the Suffrage question were cast in its favor, but not a majority of all the votes cast at the election. The supreme courts have generally held that, in so important a matter, a complete majority vote was required, but the Supreme Court of Idaho did not so hold, and woman suffrage is now established in that State. This, also, is hardly a success of sound democracy.

The subject of woman suffrage has lately been dealt with by two States that represent republican progress at its best. They are New York and Massachusetts. In the former State a Constitutional Convention in 1894 gave an impartial hearing to the subject, and decided not to submit to the people an amendment striking the word " male" from the State Constitution. Massachusetts at its

State election in 1895 asked the people to vote upon the question of extending municipal suffrage to women, and the answer was given in a heavy adverse majority. Fewer than four in one hundred women qualified to vote on the subject voted in its favor, and half a million women declined to vote at all. A majority of over 100,000 votes was cast against it by men. Utah and New York, Wyoming and Massachusetts, which States do Americans hold up as nearest their model? In which have women made most progress, and showed themselves most likely to understand their rights, privileges and duties?

During the late Presidential election the issues passed the boundary that separates party politics from patriotic faith. For months preceding that struggle the Suffrage body had conducted the most efficient campaign in its history. When the test came, California voted for sound money against repudiation, for authority against anarchy, by a small majority, and threw its ballots heavily against woman suffrage. With the enthusiastic help of its woman voters, Colorado gave its electoral voice 16 to 1 against sound money and sound Americanism. Which State can claim that its action rings truest to the stroke of honest metal in finance and in defence of national honor?

A few States have extended municipal suffrage to woman. It is generally local and restricted Only in Kansas is there full municipal suffrage. Dr. Jacobi, in her "Common Sense," says:

3

" Municipal suffrage in Kansas demands no property qualification, and its exercise therefore does not differ in the least from that required in a Presidential election." This is a mistake, for the difference is essential and illustrates the undemocratic character of woman suffrage. Municipal suffrage in Kansas, like the Territorial suffrage in Wyoming, was given by legislative act, and could be done away with by another legislative act without appeal to the people, or any change of the Constitution. It did not touch the vital question whether women, in a democracy, could form a component part of the government. Mrs. Stanton well understood that difference. Kansas had long possessed local municipal suffrage when, in 1894, the question of granting full suffrage, by constitutional amendment, was submitted to the people. Mrs. Stanton then wrote : "My hope now rests with Kansas. If that fails too, we must trust no longer to the Republican and Democratic parties, but henceforth give our money, our eloquence, our enthusiasm to a People's party that will recognize woman as an equal factor in a new civilization." There was enough leaven of republicanism working then to cause the old fighting-ground. the free-soil State, to reject the amendment by a popular majority of 35,000. To the " People's Party " in Kansas woman suffrage may look for the most striking illustration of its results. Where municipal suffrage could be secured only by constitutional enactment, and was so secured, it would differ merely in degree from presidential suffrage; but it never has been so secured in any State except those that give full constitutional suffrage. It is on a par with school suffrage, except that legislative enactment extends the vote to town and city matters.

The history of the school suffrage affords another proof of the incompatibility of republicanism and constitutional suffrage for woman. Dr. Jacobi recognizes the difference between constitutional and school suffrage when she says: " Women continually sign petitions for this privilege, till startled by the discovery that it also means something else. It means, however, in the State of New York, according to the decision of the Supreme Court, that woman can only enjoy this privilege thoroughly if empowered by constitutional amendment to vote for all officers as well as for school commissioners." The States that have refused to comply with the Suffragists' demand for the elective franchise, the most progressive States, have been first to grant school suffrage, under constitutional limits. The twenty-seven odd States that grant school suffrage have had different methods of dealing with the question, because their laws differ, but both the positive proof of its being granted, and the negative proof of its being withheld, tell the same story in regard to the fundamental principle involved. This is shown strikingly in the situation in Kansas. Women have full municipal suffrage, and the Supreme Court of that State decided that they could vote for school treasurer, which was a charter office, but could not vote for County Superintendent of Schools, because that office was provided for in the Constitution. The school suffrage may or may not have a property qualification attached. That makes no difference. The difference is the essential one between delegated power and sovereign power. The States differ so widely in their methods of dealing with municipal as well as school legislation, that only a study of the laws of each State will reveal the situation. In Ohio, in 1895, for instance, the Legislature passed a bill enabling women to vote on a municipal tax-levy, which the courts held was unconstitutional, while they granted votes on license and other local questions.

In answer to the question whether, in Massachusetts, a woman could be a member of a school committee, the Supreme Court returned the following decision in 1874: "The Constitution contains nothing relating to school committees; the office is created and regulated by statute; and the Constitution confers upon the General Court full power and authority to name and settle annually, or provide by fixed laws for naming and settling, all civil officers within the Commonwealth the election and constitution of whom are not in the Constitution otherwise provided for. The question is therefore answered in the affirmative."

The Supreme Court of New York, in 1892, held that "School Commissioners are constitutional officers within Article II. part 1 of the Constitution, and consequently the law of 1892 giving women the right to vote for them is void." The case was that of Matilda Joslyn Gage. The office of School Commissioner was created after the adoption of the Constitution, and it was therefore urged that the Constitution did not bear upon it; but the Supreme Court further decided that the law gave the Legislature the right to appoint or to elect the Commissioner; and as they had decided ·that the office should be elective, the women could not vote for that office. They vote for district-school officers under various local permissions or limitations. In a case brought to decide the right of women to vote for County Superintendent of Schools the Supreme Court of Illinois, in 1893, held that, as the office was designated in the Constitution as elective, women could not vote for it. The decision further said. "The votes for State Superintendent of Instruction, and County Superintendent, are provided for by law, and the Legislature cannot change the law. It may be that it is competent for the Legislature to provide that women who are citizens of the United States and over twenty-one may vote at elections held for school directors and other school officers not mentioned in the Constitution." Later, the Supreme Court held that women were entitled to vote for school trustees, as "no officer of the school district is mentioned in the State Constitution."

The Supreme Court of Ohio, in 1894, held that the provision of the act of April 24, 1894, conferring upon women the right to vote at elections of certain school officers, is valid, such right being within the legislative power to provide for the establishment and maintenance of public schools, and not within Article V. part 1, of the Constitution, which limits the right to male citizens. Judge Shauck says : "The whole subject of the public schools is delegated to the Assembly. As the common-school organization is wholly a creation of the Legislature, it is in the power of the Legislature to determine the qualifications of an elector and office-holder in it." In upholding his ruling, he cited similar decisions from the Supreme Courts of Illinois, Kansas, Nebraska, Massachusetts, Michigan, and Iowa.

This rapid survey suggests, it seems to me, that, instead of being "a legitimate outgrowth of the fundamental principles of our government," woman suffrage is really incompatible with true republican forms. Pre-civilized conditions, aristocratic tendencies, the forces that would destroy government—these appear to be its natural allies. We must study more closely its connection with representative government the better to comprehend this portentous truth.

# CHAPTER III.

THE writers of the "History of Woman Suffrage" give the following account of the founding of their Association. In July, 1848, Elizabeth Cady Stanton, Lucretia Mott, Martha C. Wright, and Ann McClintock issued an unsigned call for a convention, which was asked to consider the social, civil, and religious condition and rights of woman; and in preparation for the meeting, they wrote a "Declaration of Sentiments," which was adopted by the assembly. They say, in describing the writing of this declaration:—"The reports of Peace, Temperance, and Anti-Slavery conventions were examined, but all alike seemed too tame and pacific for the inauguration of a rebellion such as the world had never before seen. We knew women had wrongs, but how to state them was the difficulty, and this was increased from the fact that we ourselves were fortunately organized and conditioned. . . . After much delay, one of the circle took up the Declaration of 1776, and read it aloud with spirit and emphasis, and it was at once decided to adopt the historic document, with some slight changes. Knowing that women must

39

have more to complain of than men under any circumstances possibly could, and seeing the Fathers had eighteen grievances, a protracted search was made through statute books, church usages, and the customs of society to find that exact number."

In such solemnly puerile fashion did they work out a travesty on one of the most august utterances ever penned. A young man who was present remarked: " Your grievances must be grievous indeed when you are obliged to go to books in order to find them out." He might have added, " And they must be false indeed when you have to found most of your charges on dead-letter statutes and outgrown usages and customs."

The Preamble of their Declaration reads: "When, in the course of human events, it becomes necessary for one portion of the family of man to assume among the people of the earth a position different from that which they have hitherto occupied, but one to which the laws of nature and of nature's God entitle them, a decent respect to the opinions of mankind requires that they should declare the causes that impel them to such a course."

The declaration is as follows: " We hold these truths to be self-evident: That all men and women are created equal; that they are endowed by their Creator with certain inalienable rights; that among these are life, liberty and the pursuit of happiness; that to secure these rights governments are instituted, deriving their just powers

from the consent of the governed. Whenever any
form of government becomes destructive of these
ends, it is the right of those who suffer from it to
refuse allegiance to it, and to insist upon the institution of a new government, laying its foundation on such principles, and organizing its powers
in such form, as to them shall seem most likely to
effect their safety and happiness. Prudence, indeed, will dictate that governments long established should not be changed for light and tran-
sient causes; and accordingly all experience hath
shown that mankind are more disposed to suffer,
while evils are sufferable, than to right themselves
by abolishing the forms to which they were accustomed. But when a long train of abuses and
usurpations, pursuing invariably the same object,
evinces a design to reduce them under absolute
despotism, it is their duty to throw off such government, and to provide new guards for their
future security. Such has been the patient suf-
ferance of the women under this government, and
such is now the necessity which constrains them
to demand the equal station to which they are entitled. The history of mankind is a history of
repeated injuries and usurpations on the part of
man toward woman, having in direct object the
establishment of an absolute tyranny over her.
To prove this, let facts be submitted to a candid
world." Then follows a categorical parody of the
eighteen grievances, which will be duly considered
in this and later chapters.

After thirty years of Suffrage effort, the leaders say that this instrument contained all that the most radical have ever claimed. The Fathers of the Revolution say in their Preamble : " When, in the course of human events, it becomes necessary for one people to dissolve the political bands which have connected them with another, and to assume among the powers of the earth the separate and equal station to which the laws of nature and of nature's God entitle them, a decent respect to the opinions of mankind requires that they should declare the causes which impel them to the separation." The Mothers of the Woman's Rebellion say : " When, in the course of human events, it becomes necessary for one portion of the family of man to assume among the people of the earth a position different from that which they have hitherto occupied, but one to which the laws of nature and of nature's God entitle them, a decent respect for the opinions of mankind requires that they should declare the causes that impel them to such a course." The strained and ridiculous attitude produced by ignoring the essential difference between a political movement and a sex movement is visible in every line, and yet that instinct which finds for a new cause its appropriate channel never carried more truly than in this presentment of the ultimate purpose of woman suffrage. The Fathers were met to dissolve the relations that bound their land politically to a foreign power, and to form a separate and equal nation.

The Mothers were met to dissolve the relations that bound their sex politically to man, and to form a separate and equal sex organization. The Fathers proposed to free men, women, and children from the yoke of England. The Mothers proposed to free women and girls from the yoke of men. It is suggestive to consider the " slight changes," between the two Declarations.

The Fathers of the Revolution begin their protest by saying: "We hold these truths to be self-evident :— That all men are created equal, that they are endowed by their Creator with certain inalienable rights; that among these are life, liberty and the pursuit of happiness." The Mothers of the Woman's Rebellion add nothing to the meaning, but detract greatly from the force of its expression, when in their parody they say : "We hold these truths to be self-evident: That all men and women are created equal, and are endowed by their Creator with certain inalienable rights ; that among these are life, liberty, and the pursuit of happiness." These women of all in America were the first to belittle themselves by seeming to assume that in a revolutionary document that was promulgated to declare a determination to wrest from tyranny the liberty that was an inalienable right for all, they and their sex were excluded because the generic term " man " was employed in relation to another inalienable right, which was about to be set forth,—that of revolution against intolerable tyranny. The

Americans who framed that instrument would
have been the last men in the world to assert that
women were not the equals of men.  They were
not discussing abstract human or sex conditions.
They met " to institute a new government."  The
Mothers of the Woman's Rebellion had an inalienable right to meet "to institute a new government," if they believed as sincerely as did the
Fathers of the Revolution that "a long train of
abuses and usurpations, pursuing invariably the
same object, evinced a design to reduce them under
absolute despotism."  Life, liberty, and the pursuit of happiness were their natural and God-
given rights.  If they truly believed that these
were trampled upon by government, they might be
justified in revolting and attempting to form a
new government.  That they did not so believe,
seems to be proved by their statement that " they
knew that woman had wrongs, but how to state
them was the difficulty, and this was increased
from the fact that they themselves were fortunately organized and conditioned."  The Declaration of Independence meant war against the
ever-growing encroachment of despotism.  The
gauntlet was thrown down at the feet of a king
by his subjects.  The Declaration of Sentiments
meant war against the whole social order as then
constituted.  The gauntlet was thrown down at
the feet of man by those who declared him to be
a determined foe.

They had not the remotest notion of " institut-

ing a new government," far from it; they relied
upon the old government to sustain them in making their attempted "rebellion" a revolution.
Without the backing of the state's defence, they
had no expectation or hope of enforcing any new
enactment they might desire. They were gladly
consenting to be governed, in order to prove that
they withheld consent.

Should woman suffrage prevail, the foundation
principles of democracy would have to be over-
thrown and "a new government instituted" in
which the power should be delegated and not
direct, if the nation thus formed was to "assume
among the powers of the earth a separate and
equal station." The leaders of the Suffrage
movement well understood that they claimed no
inalienable right to institute a new government,
and this is again shown in another "slight change"
made by them. The first count in the suffrage
indictment against all men, but especially against
those of the American Republic, reads as follows:
"He has never permitted her to exercise her
inalienable right to the elective franchise." The
Fathers made no claim or suggestion that the
suffrage was an inalienable right, or a right at
all. Not only is there nothing to intimate that
voting was a natural right, but from that day to
this it has been the theory and the practice of our
Government to control the suffrage. The fact
that "governments were instituted among men"
for the purpose of securing inalienable rights,

proves that in the opinion of the Declarers the method of instituting a government was not in itself inalienable. Governments to secure certain inalienable rights are instituted among men, wrote Jefferson, " deriving their just powers from the consent of the governed." This was not the first government founded upon " consent of the governed." The English government had been so founded, but our fathers now refused their consent. That particular government could no longer exist for them with their consent. In their judgment, it had become destructive of the proper ends of all government, and so they proclaimed that the inalienable right to liberty made it—to use the words of the Declaration—" the right, the duty, of those who suffer from it to refuse allegiance to it, and to institute a new government."

In the New York Constitutional Convention of 1867, Mr. George William Curtis defended the proposition so to amend the Constitution as to extend the suffrage to women. In the course of his eloquent remarks he said: " The Chairman of the Committee asked Miss Anthony whether, if suffrage was a natural right, it could be denied to children? Her answer seemed to me perfectly satisfactory. She said simply, ' All that we ask is an equal and not an arbitrary regulation. If *you* have the right, *we* have it.' " To me it seems to discredit the logical powers both of Miss Anthony and of Mr. Curtis that one should have made this reply and the other should have rested content with it. That was a pertinent question, and it was not answered at all. To say "if you have the right, we have it," is not to tell whether one thinks children should have it. As a matter of fact, an agitation of "the rights of minors" arose from the discussion of "natural right," and also an agitation for "minority representation" that is continued to this day. Mr. Curtis added: "The honorable Chairman would hardly deny that to regulate the exercise of a right according to obvious reason and experience is one thing, to deny it absolutely and forever is another." To regulate a law is to abolish it, either relatively or absolutely, for some, and to maintain it for others. When the State of New York says that no alien who has not been naturalized shall vote, that no boy under twenty-one shall vote, that no person resident in one town or ward shall vote in another, that no criminal or pauper shall vote,—it acts on the natural principle of self-defence, which contravenes the dogma of a natural right of any one to the suffrage. On that principle it would be impossible for the Congress to impeach a President; to forbid, as it did, those who had been in rebellion from voting; or to deny the suffrage to a child or to any human being. Government itself becomes impossible. Judge Story, whom Suffrage writers claim as favorable to their cause on other grounds, says that the right of voting has always been treated as a granted and not a natural right, derived from and regulated by each country according to its ideas of government. Both Federal and State courts have decided again and again that there is no such thing as a natural right to suffrage.

The " consent of the governed " certainly meant something very different to our fathers, and to our statesmen, and to ourselves, from what it could mean to any other government on earth. Although the phrase itself may have been a euphemism which sprang from Jefferson's sympathy with the mighty rumblings of feeling that preceded the French Revolution, still, it was certainly meant that, so far as they could make it so, there should be vastly more consenting by popular vote than had been dreamed of in the mother country. But it did not mean that each and every individual in the state must consent to each and every law that governed him ; for not only has no government ever been instituted which derived " just powers " in that way, but none ever will be, for there never can be such unanimity. It did not mean that every individual must consent to be governed somehow, by some scheme of government ; for its laws were carefully framed so as to compel the external allegiance of those who never consent—the criminal and the anarchist. It did not mean even that consent, in the sense of agreement, was expected from a large body, or a small body, as the case might happen, of those who held views opposed to the policies that were controlling at any given time. It meant just what

Jefferson meant in that other dictum of his: "The will of the majority is the natural law of every society, and the only sure guardian of the rights of man." Together they interpret each other, and are worthy of our Declaration and our Bill of Rights.

The inalienable right to liberty in all mankind forbids the right of anarchy in any of mankind; and the question of woman suffrage, strange as it may appear, actually narrows itself down, as it seems to me, to the question whether we shall have democracy or anarchy. Democratic government is at an end when those who issue decrees are not identical with those who can enforce those decrees.

But, after all, the claim to suffrage as a natural right has been practically abandoned by those who first made that claim. Their next proposition was, that it was a universal right, springing from the necessary conditions of organized society, and so should be granted to woman as a member of that society. They say in their Declaration: "He deprived her of the first right of a citizen— the elective franchise." Chief Justice Waite of the United States Supreme Court decided that citizenship carried with it no voting power or right. The same decision has been handed down by many courts in disposing of test cases.

It seems to me quite as evident that what is now called universal manhood suffrage does not rest upon any belief by the state that this is "the first right of a citizen," because no one doubts that if

4

the time came when a majority deemed that the
preservation of the state depended upon disfran-
chising a number of voters, they would be disfranchised although they remained citizens. The
Suffrage leaders have, in theory at least, also
abandoned the claim to suffrage on the ground of
their universal right as citizens. A proof of this
is seen in the fact that at various times they have
suggested the extension of suffrage under qualification. Among the latest that I have noticed, is
an address of Mrs. Stanton's to a Suffrage Convention held in 1894, in which she proposed the
following: "Resolved, that the women of New
York petition the Legislature of the State to extend the suffrage to women on an educational
qualification." She must therefore believe that
the Legislature has the *legal* right to qualify it for
men ; and to withhold it from women is but an
extension of the right to qualify suffrage, because
it only says : " We do not consider woman citizens
qualified to be voters." Writing a year ago, Mrs.
Stanton said : " It is the duty of the educated
women of this Republic to protest against the extension of the suffrage to another man until they
themselves are enfranchised!" Thus it would
appear that Mrs. Stanton does not believe in universal suffrage. A Suffrage speaker in New York
not long ago said naïvely : " We [the women,
when enfranchised] will vote to withhold the
suffrage from the ignorant." She did not explain
what would happen if the ignorant voted not to

have the suffrage withheld ; nor did she appear to realize that she was practically admitting that the present voters have the right to withhold the suffrage from those whom *they* consider unfitted for it.

But it is not true that American women did not, and do not, " consent to be governed." They have always consented loyally and joyfully. From the time of the Boston Tea Party down to the Civil War, and in such times of peace and pros- perity as were indicated by the Columbian Ex- position, when the Government formally asked the assistance of its woman citizens, they showed their consent by their deeds, and only the suf- frage faction treated the invitation to share in the Exposition after the immemorial fashion of a dis- contented element. And the Suffragists themselves consent to be governed every time they accept the protection of the law or invoke it against a debtor ; for they thereby acknowledge its proper applica- tion to themselves if the case were reversed.

The second count in the list of political griev- ances runs : " He has compelled her to submit to laws in the formation of which she had no voice." This was not true, for the women who wrote that sentence were free to use their voices in regard to every law they desired to affect, and circumstances have proved that they were sure of being heard, and, if the law were just, and for the general good, of assisting materially to establish it. At the very time when Elizabeth Cady Stanton and

Lucretia Mott were writing that indictment
against the United States Government, Dorothea
Dix was presenting a memorial to the National
Congress asking for an appropriation of five hundred thousand acres of the public lands to endow
hospitals for the indigent insane.   That bill failed
to pass, but in 1850 another bill, which she presented, asking for ten millions of acres, passed the
House and failed in the Senate merely for want
of time to consider it.   Four years later a bill
making appropriations of the ten millions of acres
to the separate States passed both houses, and
President Pierce vetoed it, because he believed
the general Government had no constitutional
power to make such appropriations.   She then
went to the Legislatures of the States, with the
result that is so well known.   Rhode Island, Pennsylvania, New York, Indiana, Illinois, Louisiana,
and North Carolina founded lunatic asylums, and
the work was begun which is culminating in the
separation of the insane from the criminal, the
women from the men, in every town and county
of the land.   The right of petition is not only as
open to women as to men, but because of the non-
partisan character of their claims and suggestions
they find   quicker hearing.   Miss Louise Lee
Schuyler has been more successful in securing the
enactment of laws for which she presented the
need than any one politician in the State of New
York, before whose Legislature they have both
pleaded,—he with a vote which had to contend

against other votes, she with a voice that spoke the united mind of a body of philanthropic women. There was no unjust law which the Suffrage Association could not have changed during these fifty years, had it cared to try, and indeed its members make the boast that many of the changes are their own. Change and improvement of laws was not their aim. It was a vote upon changing or not changing laws that they sought for. The difference is world-wide.

The third count in the indictment runs : " He has withheld from her rights which are given to the most ignorant men—both natives and foreigners." Dr. Jacobi represented the Suffrage cause before the Special Committee of the Constitutional Convention of New York State in 1894. After drawing, in fine and truthfully glowing words, a picture of woman's progress under the institutions and laws of the United States, she said : " For the first time, all political right, privilege and power reposes undisguisedly on the one brutal fact of sex, unsupported, untempered, unalloyed by any attribute of education, any justification of intelligence, any glamour of wealth, any prestige of birth, any insignia of actual power. . . . To-day, the immigrants pouring in through the open gates of our seaport towns, the Indian when settled in severalty, the negro hardly emancipated from the degradation of two hundred years of slavery,—may all share in the sovereignty of the State. The white woman,—the woman in whose veins runs the blood of those heroic colonists who founded our country, of those women who helped to sustain the courage of their husbands in the Revolutionary War; the woman who may have given the flower of her youth and health in the service of our Civil War—that woman is excluded. To-day women constitute the only class of sane people excluded from the franchise, the only class deprived of political representation, except the tribal Indians and the Chinese." To the same effect the editors of the " Suffrage History " say: " The superiority of man does not enter into the demand for suffrage ; for in this country all men vote ; and as the lower orders of men are not superior to the higher orders of women, they must hold and exercise the right of self-government on some other ground than superiority to woman." Here it would seem that Mrs. Stanton and Miss Anthony had been thinking, but they never followed their own thought to its inevitable conclusion. Universal manhood suffrage does relieve the men of this country from the unjust aspersion the women of the Suffrage movement put upon them, that they excluded women on account of inferiority.

No native American, who by the very fact of that nativity is bound to support the Constitution of the United States, and no foreign-born citizen who has taken the oath of allegiance to it, has a right by his vote to do anything that will imperil or impede the carrying out of its principles and its commands. "The establishment of justice, the insurement of domestic tranquillity, provision for the common defence, security in the blessings of liberty to ourselves and our posterity," cannot be perfected or maintained without the present exercise and the reserve power of manhood strength. This Government laid aside all "attribute of education, or glamour of wealth, or prestige of birth," and committed its life to the keeping of its defenders. In this land, the vote *is* the "insignia of actual power," but it is only the insignia; the power to defend themselves and those who make country and home worth defending, lies with the individual defenders. To attempt to put it into the hands of those who are not physically fitted to maintain the obligations that may result from any vote or any legislative act, is to render law a farce, and to betray the trust imposed upon them by the constitution they have sworn to uphold. Universal manhood suffrage is the crowning result in the long evolution of government. Our statesmen of the Revolutionary period did not contemplate it. But stability was the thing for which they sought —the thing for which all statesmen of all times have been searching. If a government is not stable, it is of little consequence that it is full of noble ideals; and the most far-reaching thought has now grasped the idea that manhood strength is the natural and only defence of the state. This is the underlying theory of our Government, the one solid rock on which it rests. When any question of governmental policy comes up, we virtually decide it, sooner or later, by a manhood vote; and as the decision has a majority of the men of the country behind it, there is no power that can overthrow it. If we attempt to establish policies or execute laws to which a majority of the men are opposed, we throw away our one assurance of stability, and are in constant danger of revolution. Even in the comparatively brief history of our Republic, there are plentiful instances to show that a majority of men will not submit to a minority, no matter how many non-combatants are joined with that minority. To give women a position of apparent power, without its reality, would be to make our Government forever unstable.

"This is placing the Christian and civilized Government that stands as an example of peaceful progress on a foundation of brute force," cries the Suffragist. The founders of the Woman Suffrage movement apparently did not take the least account of either the military or the judicial powers that are provided for in every State constitution, as well as in the Nation's. They demanded "immediate admission to all the rights and privileges which belong to them as citizens of the United States," but said not a word about the duties, disabilities, and money loss involved in the possession of those rights and privileges. The Fathers of the Revolution closed their Declara-

tion of Independence from the tyranny of England by pledging " their lives, their fortunes and
their sacred honor " to attain it. The Mothers of
the Woman's Rebellion closed their Declaration
of Independence from the tyranny of man, and
especially from the tyranny of the United States
Government, with a pledge to distribute tracts
and hold conventions, while they depended upon
the courtesy of the tyrants to protect them in the
peaceful execution of their design. Is it any wonder that the descendants of the old heroes who
had fought their way to our liberties smiled when
the by-laws of the would-be revolt were handed
to them?

When the attention of the women was called
to the fact that force was needed, and that women
were exempt from military service and jury and
police duty, they answered that " In an age when
the wrongs of society are adjusted in the courts
and at the ballot-box, material force yields to reason and majorities." So successful has our Government been in carrying out the benign purposes
for which its heroes staked their lives, their fortunes, and their sacred honor, that in ordinary
times we see little of the strength that stands
quietly but firmly behind every law's enactment
and every poll's decision. The "strong arm" of
the law would lose its power to compel obedience
if behind the decree of judge, jury, and legislators
there was not a sheriff or a body of militia ready
to commit the unconsenting criminal to prison, or

to take care of an unruly minority. At an election, the minority do not acquiesce in the decision of the majority because the outcome of the vote has convinced them that the majority were right, and they were wrong. They have not become suddenly converted to the views of the majority. That decision, as recorded by the ballot, shows that if the minority do not keep their opinion in abeyance, there are men enough on the other side to compel them. Civilization has advanced so far that, instead of blows there are arguments in court, instead of bullets there are ballots at the polls; but the blows and the bullets must always be ready, in case the arguments and the ballots are unheeded. The physical strength that was given to man to use, like every other gift, for the good of the race, he is so using when he holds it as a *dernier ressort* for law and order.

Dr. Jacobi says, in her address, " capacity to bear arms, in fulfilment of military duty, is not, in the State of New York, reckoned among the necessary qualifications of voters." The statement is also made by other Suffragists that " numerous classes of men who enjoy political rights are exempt from military duty,—all men over forty-five, all who suffer mental or physical disability, such as the loss of an eye or a forefinger; clergymen, physicians, Quakers, school-teachers, professors, and presidents of colleges, judges, legislators, congressmen, state-prison officials, and all county, State, and National officers; fathers, brothers, or sons having certain relatives dependent upon them for support, all of these summed up in every State would make millions who may be exempted, and therefore there is no force in the plea that if women vote they must fight." It is not true that any class of voters is exempt. The State, regulating that matter as it regulates the age and residence of voters, as long as it has more defenders than it needs for immediate use, makes demand upon the youngest or strongest, but if it needs them all, then all must serve. Again, all, whether young or old, perfect or imperfect, must be reckoned with as elements in making up the count. Lawless men do not exempt themselves from riot and rebellion because they are lame or over forty-five. In the South, during the Rebellion, there were few indeed who did not serve in some capacity. If there were blind and aged men enough to make a real difference in majorities, Americans would quickly see the propriety of doing as some republics that have to stand with arms more " at attention " have done, and exclude them from the vote.

But, suppose all those mentioned were really exempt, how would that apply to women ? If a like number were counted out, there would still be a goodly array, from the maiden of twenty-one to the matron of forty-five, from which to draw. Mrs. Stanton and Miss Anthony write: " Women have led armies in all ages, have held positions in the army and navy for years in disguise, have fought, bled, and died on the battle-field in our late war." The isolated occasions on which they have done so are not such as to commend the practice, neither do the Suffragists propose seriously to commend it. Dr. Jacobi, in her address before the Committee of the Constitutional Convention, says: " We do not admit that exemption from military duty is a concession of courtesy, for which women should be so grateful as to refrain from asking for anything else. The military functions performed by men, and so often perverted to most atrocious uses, have never been more than the equivalent for the function of child-bearing imposed by nature upon women. It is not a fanciful nor sentimental, it is an exact and just equivalent. The man who exposes his life in battle, can do no more than his mother did in the hour she bore him. And the functions of maternity persist, and will persist, to the end of time,—while the calls to arms are becoming so faint and rare that three times since the Revolutionary War, an entire generation of men has grown up without having heard them."

This question of military service is not a question of equivalent at all—sentimental or otherwise; it is a question of the actual service, and as to the service to the state given by women in bearing sons, the men work not only to support those sons but to support also their mothers and sisters, and that far beyond the child-bearing age of the mother. -

As to the rareness of the calls, I read of seven wars since the Revolution, and three insurrections, not counting the riots and strikes at Chicago, Homestead, Brooklyn, and in the mountains in the West. Dr. Jacobi said in an article in the " New York Sun," two years ago, " We do not vote for war." That appears like a quibble, for we vote for what brings, or may bring it; but neither is it exact in fact. Three times, at least, in our history men have deposited their ballots in the box, knowing that the result meant peace or war. These were at the second election of Madison in 1812, the election of Polk in 1844, and that most solemn of all the acts of our countrymen, the second election of President Lincoln. There have been other elections in which war issues were linked with the decisions, but in a less direct way.

The same writer says also, " The will of the majority rules, for the time being, not, as has been crudely asserted, because it possesses the power, by brute force, to compel the minority to obey its behests ; but because, after ages of strife, it has been found more convenient, more equitable, more conducive to the welfare of the state, that the minority should submit, until, through argument and persuasion, they shall have been able to win over the majority. Now that this stage in the evolution of modern society has been reached, it has become possible for women to demand their share also in the expression of the public opinion that is to rule. They could not claim this while it was necessary to defend opinions by arms; but this is no longer either necessary or expected."

How long is it since this comfortable state of things was evolved? Has England consented to it? In view of Venezuela and the Monroe Doctrine it would be necessary to have her. Has Spain mentioned her resignation of a right to appeal to arms in case she was not pleased with the conduct of our Government in regard to Cuba? Does the Sultan know about it, so that in case we see a good fair fighting chance to help the Armenians he will understand that the ages of strife are over, and that persuasion has been found more equitable and convenient than a resort to arms? And the Czar, and the erratic German Emperor, are they in the evolutionary agreement? Force is just what men are able to make it. It is not brutish unless it is brutishly used. There is as much force in the world to-day as there ever has been, but it is better applied. It is the object of a Christian civilization to persuade more and more men to come to the defence of good against evil in forms of government. Despotism and absolutism are corrupt uses of force. Republicanism and a constitutional government are its nobler uses. But the force is still behind them, or there would be no power to continue such liberal forms. During the first Republic, Marathon and Thermopylæ saved the principle of Western democracy against Oriental despotism, Salamis and

Platæa saved Greek letters and Greek art to the continents that were yet to be. Christianity changed the motive but not the method in evolution; and, finally in the last great Republic, the American Revolution proclaimed liberty of thought, the war of 1812 secured American independence, while, beside the wandering Antietam and on the field of Gettysburg " green regiments went to their graves like beds " that the Union might live, and that human slavery might die. Manhood force, led by intelligence and goodness, is the bulwark of that maternity that must persist if heroes are to be. Dr. Jacobi's admission that women could not claim the vote while it was necessary to defend opinions by arms, is a vital one, for it contravenes her entire argument.

Another plea of the Suffrage leaders is that "men send substitutes, and so could women." The answer in regard to exempt classes will apply here also, because in case of need both substitute and substituter are obliged to serve. During our Civil War the fact that a man had sent a substitute did not prevent him from being called in the next draft. The state claims both men as its defenders. But whom do the women propose to substitute? Other women? No, they propose to substitute men! The Suffragists seriously suggest that half the population, exempted by nature from military duty, shall become organic members of a government whose reliance, embodied in every constitution, is upon the ability

and the willingness of its organic members to do
military duty in defence of those constitutions,
and that this exempted half may have it as their
sole office, in case of war, to vote when and where
the lives, the fortunes, and the sacred honor of
those other organic members shall be laid down
or imperilled. Suffragists seem to forget, when
they boast of Joan of Arc, that the army she led
was masculine.

The English socialist, Mrs. Stanton Blatch,
daughter of Elizabeth Cady Stanton, in her addresses in this country two years ago, said:
" Woman is not protected through chivalry, but
because the men know that to put women to the
front is national suicide. Woman's part in war
is not to wail or weep, but to furnish the army
for the future." Then there is to be an army for
the future! Was there no "national suicide"
when over three million men were "put to the
front" in the Rebellion, and more than five hundred thousand, North and South, laid down their
lives, so that through the veins of this generation
runs none of the gallant blood they spilled?
Shall the fathers, and possible fathers, be the only
ones to die, if the mothers and betrothed proclaim
themselves no longer desirous of being protected
by such high sacrifice? If women cease to " weep
and wail," will men not cease to be willing to be
" furnished by them to the army?"

> " At any cost one good is cheap—
> The soldiers die lest women weep;

And this reward is great and high—
The women weep that soldiers die."

Women and soldiers cannot transpose their work. The duty of each to the Republic is equally " great and high ; " but in order to be done it must be kept distinct as now.

But all this is subordinate to the real, vital question. In the passages just quoted, the writers make an error that is made so persistently by all Suffragists whenever the argument of force is alluded to, that it seems necessary to repeat the explanation. They assume that this argument, briefly stated, is : The men do the fighting, therefore they ought to be rewarded with the ballot. That is *not* the argument; it is no matter of reward. The argument, briefly stated, is this: Stability is one of the highest virtues that any government can possess, and perhaps the most necessary. It can have no stability if it issues decrees that it cannot enforce. · The only way to avoid such decrees is, to make sure that behind every law and every policy adopted stands a power so great that no power in the land can overthrow it. The only such power possible consists of a majority of the men. Therefore, the only safe thing for the Government to do is, to carry out the ascertained will of a majority of the men. This does not always secure ideally good laws, but it does secure stability and avoids revolution. The majority may blunder ; but they are the only power that can correct their own blunders.

5 /

But war does not call for the only form of public service. There are others provided for in the National and State constitutions, which are constant and exacting. They are jury, police and militia duty. When a boy reaches twenty-one the law says to him, "You are my servant." If a fire breaks out, the foreman can legally lay his hand on the boy's shoulder, and say, "Help to put out this conflagration." When the law is broken, the sheriff can say to him, "Help me make this arrest." When a turn of the judicial wheel brings out his name, he must serve the state on a jury; if a riot occurs, he can be called out to quell it; and if a war arises, he can be drafted to fight against the country's enemies. There is not a single act of defence to which the voter was subjected by law when the Constitution was framed, to which he is not subject now, and subject because he is a voter. The vote is not given to him as a reward for standing ready to give this service to the state; it is a recognition by the state that, as he must stand ready to defend it, he should assist in establishing the laws which it may call upon him to enforce. As he has assisted to frame them, he cannot refuse to defend them. Woman's only relation to this defence is that of beneficiary, and therefore her relation to the laws with which that defence is associated must be one of advice and not of control. Fortunately for her, advice may prove sometimes to be control of the most satisfactory kind, a kind that admits of mental power and does not exact physical.

The statement is further made by Suffragists that "though woman needs the protection of one man against his whole sex, in pioneer life, in threading her way through a lonely forest, on the highway, or in the streets of a metropolis on a dark night, she sometimes needs, too, the protection of all men against this one. But even if she could be sure, as she is not, of the ever-present, all-protecting power of one strong arm, that would be weak indeed compared with the subtle, all-pervading influence of just and equal laws for all women. Hence woman's need of the ballot, that she may hold in her own right hand the weapon of self-protection and defence." The possession of the ballot has not been able to secure for men "the subtle and all-pervading influence of just and equal laws," and despite his holding the ballot in his own hand, man has had to hold also a more apparent weapon if he visit a striker's camp or meddle with an anarchist riot. Something more tangible than protective influence is needed to make the public streets of this city safe for women in broad daylight. Again, they say that "Wisdom would suggest division of labor in peace as well as in war." Wisdom would have no chance to make such a suggestion, if women attempted to do the same work as do men, in the same way. There is true division of labor now, in peace as well as in war.

Suffragists mention as a final indignity the extension of the suffrage to the negro. Their protest only serves to suggest another forcible illustration of the fact that law and the enforcement of law may be different things. The suffrage is not extended to the negro. The Congress of the United States voted that it should be so extended; and while the Government stood behind his vote with its military power, the negro voted. But no one pretends that he has done so, to any practical extent, since that time. Unarmed, the negro finds that he cannot enforce his own vote against the will of white men armed to the teeth. The " all-pervading influence of just and equal laws " cannot enforce it for him. Would the women be any better off, if the men chose that they should not exercise the vote? Who would enforce it?

This fact and argument show how little arbitration has to do with the practical decision concerning suffrage. Suffrage writers and speakers harp upon the thought that arbitration will take the place of force. That method of settling disputes cannot come too quickly, but it has not come yet. It has no real bearing on the organization of the state as resting upon the civil and military service of its citizens. England consented to arbitrate with the powerful United States, but refused to arbitrate with defenceless Nicaragua in a far less important matter. Congress has seriously considered exterminating the remnant of the beautiful herd of seals that once played in our Northern Pacific waters, because British subjects have continued, in violation of the Arbitration treaty, to kill the animals with cruelty. Behind arbitration, as behind all law and order, military power must always stand and must sometimes be used.

One more proof that the vote is not the real power, but only its insignia, lies in the fact that legislation has not been able to put an end to strikes and riots. Laws that forbid them are passed with all due form ; but when they come, as come they do, the reading of the riot act is suspended and the regiments are ordered to Chicago, or Buffalo, or Brooklyn, or Homestead, or Cripple Creek, or Cleveland, or the Indian country. The force of those bodies was not " brutal," it was physical power obeying mental ; and unless mental power can command physical, there is no way in which mental power can enforce its decrees in government. There are now facing us tremendous moral issues, which presage tremendous struggles ; and a very notable example of the dangers that would attend woman suffrage is suggested by them. If women had the power to create a numerical majority when there was a majority of the law's natural and only defenders against them, they might soon precipitate a crisis that would lead to bloodshed, which they would be powerless either to prevent or to allay. Would the majority of men submit to the minority of men associated with non-combatants? American history furnishes no reason for supposing that they would. The Dorr War in Rhode Island is a case in point, in local matters. I am neither an alarmist nor a believer in war as a panacea ; but if we discuss this subject at all, we must discuss it with facts and not fancies in our minds.

Dr. Jacobi again says, in her book : " It may be said, for it has been said, that the objection to seeing a vote of seven hundred men overcome by a coalition of three hundred men with eight hundred women, lies in the fact that the defeated minority knows, if it had a free hand and was allowed to use fisticuffs, it could pound into a jelly a majority composed so largely of women. It would feel, therefore, sullen, restive, and justly indignant, that it should be prohibited from using this power and obliged to submit to a merely nominal force and supremacy."

The objection to seeing seven hundred men defeated by a coalition of three hundred men with eight hundred women, lies in the fact that the defeated minority knows that it *has* a free hand, and that nothing less than eight hundred men could prevent it from using its physical power, were it so inclined. Only a force and supremacy that was real, and not nominal, could make it to submit. The rhetorical trick of belittling the matter by speaking of it as " fisticuffs " will not pass in this discussion. When the South Carolina negroes on election day looked into the rifle-barrels of the Red-shirt clubs, it was no matter of fisticuffs.

When every statesman in our country was eagerly seeking a peaceful solution of the Hayes-Tilden dispute, it was not fisticuffs that they feared. When the Dostie convention was broken up and its leaders murdered in New Orleans, it was not by means of fisticuffs. When the Chicago anarchists threw their bomb into the ranks of the policemen in Haymarket Square, they were not playing at fisticuffs. When the railway strikers in Pittsburg stopped the trains, "killed" the locomotives, and burned the freight, there was no fisticuffs about it. And when a Southern minority refused to abide by the result of the election of 1860, and the Northern majority shouldered muskets and went down and compelled them to, not the most flippant writer would have thought of calling it fisticuffs. All these are simply readily recalled instances of the necessity for power in the enforcement of law.

She goes on to say : "But is it only in such a hypothetical case that a minority would know it could, if allowed to resort to physical force, shiver to fragments the majority ? The burly brakemen in railroad strikes would, probably, in a fair hand-to-hand encounter, be much bested over all the stockholders of the road,—weakened, not only because they included women in their midst, but also by sedentary habits and predominately indoor occupations. Why do they not try this way of settling their difficulties? Why do not the classes in England, who still remain entirely disfran-

chised, and with whom rests so much physical
strength, drop their fists into the balance as
Brennus did his sword, and cut short the futile,
womanish discussion ? The answer is ready in
every one's mouth. It is not that it cannot
be done, but that, on the whole, people are
all agreed that it is best it should not be done.
It is not that physical force is respected less,
but that mental force is respected more."

I reply that both these things have been attempted over and over again, and the agreement
of all the wise and good people that it is best that
it should not be done cannot prevent it. Behind
the burly brakemen who have seized the train,
and the stockholders to whom it lawfully belongs,
there lies a power greater than all the brakemen
and stockholders together. We call it the power
of law. It is, in fact, the power of a sovereign
people, who, having made that law, are able to
enforce it against the breakers of it. It is necessary, in the discussion of this point, to have
clearly in mind the difference between sovereign
power and delegated power. When a member of
a stock company attends the annual meeting and
casts one vote for every share that he holds, he
is exercising delegated power. The sovereign
people, acting through their representatives in the
legislature, have delegated to the company the
power to regulate its affairs in this way, and
guaranteed to each shareholder this privilege.
Should a combination of some of the shareholders

attempt to prevent one from exercising it, he would appeal to the court, and behind the court stands the power of the people, many times larger than any stock company that exists. On the other hand, when men go to the polls on election day, they exercise, not delegated, but sovereign, power. There is no greater power, above and beyond themselves, to regulate their actions. The enfranchised classes in England do drop their fists into the balance, and, as a result, we have seen the extensions of suffrage that marked the years 1832 and 1848, and the reason some classes are still unfranchised is, that the monarchy that wills their unfranchisement has, as yet, more power at command than those who would enfranchise them. Mental and moral force is more respected with every rolling year, because those who respect it have been able to obtain control of the physical power that can force its decrees upon those who do not respect it.

The third count in the indictment is : " Having deprived her of the first right of a citizen, the elective franchise, thereby leaving her without representation in the halls of legislation, he has oppressed her on all sides." As, in securing the exact number of grievances mentioned by the Fathers, the Mothers were compelled to string out their distresses somewhat, I will quote the next count in the indictment, and consider these two together. "After depriving her of all rights as a married woman, if single, and the owner of property, he has taxed her to support a government which recognized her only when her property could be made profitable to it."

The many-sided oppression, and the deprivation as a married woman, belong in other chapters. The remaining portions of the two counts may be summed up under the familiar cry: "No taxation without representation." What did that just accusation mean when our fathers uttered it in regard to English tyranny? Did they mean that their property was taxed, and they had no redress? The phrase originated with Patrick Henry, who read to the Virginia House of Burgesses the decision gleaned from a study of "Coke upon Lyttleton," that "Englishmen living in America had all the rights of Englishmen living in England, the chief of which was, that they could only be taxed by their own representatives," and on that was founded the resolution adopted by them that the colonies could not be lawfully taxed in a body in which they were not represented; for the colonies, as well as individuals, had no vote in Parliament. They meant that their property could not be so taxed, and they meant far more. The more that they meant was embodied by Jefferson in the first draft of the Declaration of Independence, when he said: "Can any one reason be assigned why a hundred and sixty thousand *electors* in the island of Great Britain should give law to four million in the States of America?" John Hancock meant that and more when he said: "Burn Boston and make John Hancock a beggar, if the public good requires it." He was offering his taxed property to defend the liberties of the four millions against the hundred and sixty thousand electors. The refusal of the majority to be ruled longer by the minority was the main motive of determination not to submit. But at that time all voting was connected with a tax on property, and so was the suffrage established by these men. And under those property-tax laws women who held property could vote. It was when taxation ceased to go with representation, that the women ceased to vote. There is now no connection between taxation of property and representation. When people were allowed votes in proportion to the amount of property they held, and could vote in different counties and States, there was a connection, and that law gave the rich man more voting power than the poor man. But all aristocratic qualification was done away with, and the government came to rely solely on the strength of individual men for its defence, instead of upon men and women with money enough to raise soldiery.

There is a money tax levied on the property of men and women alike; and in return for the payment of this tax the property of both men and women is made secure against unlawful injury. In order to make it secure, the state lays, upon men alone, a service tax, and with that tax goes representation, or the vote. This service tax does not fall upon woman, and it cannot be demanded of her; so it is not true that "Man has taxed her to support a government which recognizes her only when her property can be made profitable to it." He has, in return for the money tax, so guarded her property through the service tax on men that it is of profit to her, which without that guard it could not be.

The tax on property is collected from that of minors and unnaturalized citizens, resident or non-resident, and to all these classes, as well as to non-voting women, is given the right of petition and legal redress of whatever sort. The men do not have "equal rights" in regard to public control of their taxable property, if equal rights means that each man shall be able to say what shall be done to, or with, or about, the property on which he pays taxes. The penniless voter can have as much to say as to whether a railroad shall cross the lands of a millionaire as the millionaire himself. At every town election the minority are unheeded, so far as the vote goes, and women with property interests would be no better off if they secured votes in the only way they can be secured—one voice, one vote.

· Lydia Maria Child said, in a letter reprinted in the Woman's edition of "The Rochester Post-Express" in 1896: "I reduce the argument to very simple elements. I pay taxes for property of my own earning and saving, and I do not believe in taxation without representation. As for representation by proxy, that savors too much of the plantation system, however kind the master may be. I am a human being, and every human being has a right to a voice in the laws which claim authority to tax him, to imprison him, or to hang him."

Not only has every human being in the United States a right to a voice in the laws that claim authority to tax him, imprison him, or hang him, but he can exercise that right in all portions of the United States where the laws that claim this authority are able to enlist sufficient physical force to execute the authority claimed. Where they have not that power, neither the voter nor the non-voter has any redress against violence offered to property or limb or life. Gerrymanders and lynchings in many parts of our land prove the truth of this. The mastery of men who abide by and execute law is not a mastery over women for the sake of the spoils of taxation or the disposal of life, but the mastery over lawlessness everywhere in order that tax-payers of either sex, native or alien, voters or non-voters, may be enabled to have that voice in the laws which, as human beings, is their right. As to the "vote by proxy," if Mrs. Child could not trust her husband, her son, her brother, or best friend to look after her interests, she certainly could not trust the carrying out of her wish, as expressed in her vote, to the men who cast in their ballots by her side.

In return for the taxes paid, women get just what

men get,—namely, roads, gas, water, schools, etc. The women who have refused to pay their taxes because they did not vote, have been treated with a leniency that proves the courtesy of the law-enforcers. They would have made short work with men who were non-voters, who had tried the same tactics. When a man's vote is challenged and refused, he does not dream of saying: "I shall not pay my tax," and the assessor never inquires whether he votes or desires to vote. The men in the District of Columbia do not find their unfranchised condition assuaged by the smallness of their account with the assessor. Neither do they realize or believe that they are governed without their consent, or exempt from police or military duty. This is a striking proof that the vote is not a reward for service. They are male American citizens, over twenty-one years old, and they must contribute service simply and solely for that reason. This is the price they pay for established order.

For, after all, what is government, and what are taxation and representation? When and how did society consent to be governed? When did it agree to be taxed and to be represented? The awful story of history, from the slaying of Abel to the slaughter of half a million men in the War of Secession, is the answer. It never did agree, it has not yet agreed. The struggle of civilization is the effort to make it agree. Implanted in the bosom of man by his Maker is the belief in his individual freedom, of worship as concerns that Maker, of protection as concerns man. Side by side with that, was implanted the principle of surrender of a part of that freedom for just cause. There came a time when men said: "Let us use arguments instead of force in these decisions," and some form of vote was instituted. With this they fought and voted by turns, as they set up or knocked down emperors, kings, popes, and presidents. War has been changed by progress because man has changed; but main strength to drive home the truths gained on the moral battlefield is still the power behind the throne of the National conscience, even in this enlightened land.

Though the Mothers of the Rebellion did not ask, and apparently did not think of asking, to share the military duties incident to suffrage, we must discuss it, if we are to consider the subject thoroughly. To be a voting citizen, is to be a possible soldier citizen. There is no way of fulfilling the moral part of the duty, and leaving unfulfilled the physical, and it is cowardly to attempt it. So the question comes, could American women be soldiers? They could, for a few in disguise were in service during the War of Secession. Titled women of Europe are honorary officers; but this playing soldier is a relic of Middle-Age chivalry. Women can be seriously destructive; but no one will claim that organized military duty is really practicable for them.

And the suffrage proposition does not look to anything of the kind.  The Suffragists demand equal vote in sending their fathers, brothers, sons, husbands, and lovers to the military field of action, and propose to be absolutely exempt from equal share in the duty that that vote now lays upon male voters.  Before the law there could be no distinction of duty on account of race, sex, or previous condition of servitude.  The " emancipated " woman would be emancipated into that which the Declaration of Independence expressly called for, " the right and privilege of the people to bear arms."

The constitution of Utah says that the State militia is to consist of " able-bodied males," and I have not yet heard that the women who vote there have insisted that the word " male" be struck out of that clause of the Constitution.  By no means, every woman expects to be exempt. After women had succeeded in getting the framers of the constitution of every State to strike out the word " male," from its voting qualification, they would expect them to insert the word " male" in mentioning the service qualification.  O Equality, where is thine equal for granting privilege ! Such chivalry, it would seem, is an insult to the power and intelligence of the women of Utah, who celebrated their " enfranchisement " by a convention to favor the free coinage of silver, 16 to 1, and whose behavior on that occasion was, to say the least, boyish.  The tax upon time and

strength, and the money loss of citizen service,
Suffrage leaders did not once allude to.   They did
not, and do not, propose to pay even a double
money tax on account of expected exemption.
Little as this would have availed to meet the
actual situation, it would have shown their good
will, and some comprehension of justice, while
they talked of an absurd and intangible "right."

But, it might be said, "Utah did insert such a
clause into her constitution, and so could other
States.   It is, after all, common sense that rules,
and men can legislate what they please."   The
law passed by Utah, which provided that "male
voters must be tax-payers, while female voters
need not be," was decided to be unconstitutional,
and this one also may well be.   At the end
of Utah's Constitution, as of every other, and
of every bill that is passed, occurs or is understood something like this  sentence from the United States Constitution:  "The  Congress shall
have power to enforce this article by appropriate
legislation."   Is it the "appropriate legislation"
that gives to Congress, or to any other body, the
power to enforce the article decided upon by a
majority?   We know that it is not.   It is the
men who can enforce it if it is disobeyed.   Every
day we see that some laws are "dead letters,"
not because the legislation appropriate to their
enforcement was not perfect, but because they
are not enforced.   When Mr. Roosevelt became
Chairman  of the  Police  Commission  there had
6

been for some time a bill, duly legislated, for the enforcement of the Sunday closing of liquor saloons
in New York city. But the saloons had not been
closed. Mr. Roosevelt summoned the police, and
proceeded to enforce the law. If they had refused, the militia stood behind them. Do you
say, " Very well, if Miss Willard had been Chairman of the Commissioners she could have done
the same." There would have been this great
difference. Mr. Roosevelt himself was as much
subject to serve at the call of the law, as were the
policemen. He was not a dictator merely, he
was part and parcel of the strength that he in-
voked. The reason for obedience rested on the
same ground in each case—service in which each
stood equal. It is a specious form of mistake to
suppose that " men can legislate just what they
wish to." They can legislate only what the
majority decrees, and they can legislate effectively
only what they have power to enforce. Had the
saloon-keepers refused to obey Miss Willard, not
she, but Mr. Roosevelt and other men would have
had to enforce the law.

It is absurd in itself, and annoying to Suffrage
advocates, to talk about military duty for woman.
Her very nature forbids it. So it is, and so it
does, and therefore it is equally absurd to talk
about her attempting to assume duties whose very
nature forbids their being done by her. Were
voting only a matter of obtaining the *opinion* of
women on matters that concern the country, or

concern them (and all matters that concern the country concern them), all precedent gathered from the treatment of American women by American men goes to prove that no urging would have been required to secure for them as large a measure of suffrage as was consistent with their duties and their desires.

In 1879 an earnest discussion on Woman Suffrage was held in the legislature of Massachusetts. Four propositions were pending. The first was that a constitutional amendment should be submitted to the people, which, if accepted, would decree to women full suffrage. Thomas Wentworth Higginson, Lucy Stone and William Lloyd Garrison argued the case for the women. Col. Higginson said that if ability to fight were made the test of voting " a large proportion of men, especially of professional men, would be disfranchised. The report of the Surgeon-General of the United States showed that of the thousand clergymen who volunteered or were drafted during the war. 945 were declared to be unfit for service. Of the lawyers who volunteered or were drafted, 650 were rejected, and of the physicians, 745." He added, " You must go down to the mechanics and laborers before you can find a class of men a majority of whom will fulfil this requirement. Of the clergymen who preach that woman suffrage is wrong because women can do no military duty, only one twentieth would themselves be accepted for such service. There is but one class of men better fitted than mechanics for military service, and that is the prize-fighting class, and therefore the constituency which sent John Morrissey to Congress was the only constituency that ever carried out this idea to the end." Col. Higginson, who played a gallant part in the Civil War, should have remembered what poor fighting material the country found in such men as formed the constituency of John Morrissey. The regiment of Zouaves raised in New York City by Billy Wilson, the pugilist, was found to be so mischievous, as well as worthless, that it was shipped to the Dry Tortugas in order to rid the army of a pest. On the other hand, many of the most gallant as well as most orderly soldiers came from dry-goods stores and apothecary shops. The pugilists and roughs are the very ones that are good for nothing as soldiers ; they belong to the class that makes soldiery necessary.

When Col. Higginson can use such logic, it is no wonder that women have repeated the argument. The question was not whether, because certain men who were naturally looked upon by the Government as its defenders, and as such were called upon to fight, proved physically unable, but whether the Government had a right, because of its very existence, to call upon those men, and in case of need, to say to them " Put yourself into physical condition for this service." If it had such a right, by what law under the constitution of the United States could Lucy Stone ask to vote and not expect to have her military fitness inquired into, and be asked to put herself into physical condition for it?

Recalling the action of her grandfather, she, better than some other women, might have realized the necessity of force for government. Her defiant spirit might well have descended from that ancestor who led four hundred men in Shays's Rebellion, when, in the State before whose tribunal she was speaking, he assisted in preventing court sessions, and swelled the ranks of the rioters who were decrying taxes and calling for fiat money, in a land that was impoverished and was struggling for a sound financial standing after a war that had been waged to guarantee the blessings of freedom to her and to her children.

As a matter of fact, many of those men whom Col. Higginson referred to as deemed unfit, did go into immediate training, and " muscular Christianity " would now present to the Surgeon-General a different showing. It was one of the surprising things, in a statistical way, to find that city-bred boys stood the marching and exposure of the Civil War campaigns better than their country brothers, and that the yard-stick turned into as effective a sword as the pruning-hook. Garrison, who maintained for so many years that men should not vote because the government was founded on force, had the grace not to speak on this phase of the question, but he said it was cruel that women should be disfranchised and classed with paupers, idiots, and criminals. Senator Hayes asked him if there was no "difference between a person who was disfranchised and one who never had been enfranchised?" and added that "he could see no argument for woman suffrage in the proposition that certain classes of men were not permitted to vote." Neither can I.

The argument for woman suffrage which bases it upon a fancied grouping of women with the vile and brainless element in the country, appears to me to be at once the weakest and the meanest of all. When the United States Government invited its woman citizens to share in making the Columbian Exposition the most wondrous pageant of any age, they responded from every town and hamlet by sending of their best. But the national Suffrage Association, as its official exhibit, gave a picture of the expressive face of Miss Willard surrounded by ideal heads of a pauper, an idiot, and a criminal, with a legend recording their belief that it was with these that American men placed American women. So false a picture must have taught the thoughtful gazers the opposite lesson from the one intended. It could have told them that the United States Government had at least guarded one trust with sacred care. The pauper was excluded from the ballot as not being worthy to share with freemen the honor of its defence. The unfortunate was excluded by an inscrutable decree of Providence. The criminal was excluded as being dangerous to society. The women were exempt from the ballot because it was for their special safety that a free ballot was to be exercised, from which the pauper and the criminal must be excluded. They were the ones who have given to social life its meaning and its moral, the ones who give to civic life its highest value.

The authors of the " History" so often referred to, in answer to the claim that " government needs force behind it, and those who make the laws must execute them, and a woman could not be a sheriff or policeman," say : " Woman might not fill these offices as men do, but might far more effectively guard the morals of society and the sanitary conditions of our cities." A "moral guard" might be an excellent thing to ward off the ghosts in a country burying-ground, but would hardly prove effective against the riot of a Tammany mob on the night of an exciting election. It is absurd to speak in such fashion of work that is needed every hour. The crust of our civilization is very thin—how thin, the nation learned during the campaign just passed. Like a tempest from a clear sky, or one of their own cyclones, burst an influence from a portion of the West and South, that would have overturned the Government. Men struck fanatically and misguidedly at the integrity of the Supreme Court, at the power of the United States to hold jurisdiction over its own public affairs where they conflicted with State right, at the currency that gave the country ability to be honest at home and abroad, at the prosperity and honor of every citizen.

Fifteen years ago Suffrage leaders wrote in view of the wonderful advance of woman: "The broader demand for political rights has not commanded the thought its merits and dignity should have secured." If this was true, it had not been for lack of having the demand pressed home upon Congress and upon every State and Territorial legislature (save in most of the South), in season and out of season, by every device known to politics, as well as by a steady and impetuous flow of literature and petitions. How have these bodies answered this long appeal? It would take too much time and space, even were it of value, to follow the course of its ups and downs through all these years, but I mention first the fact that no State in New England has ever granted constitutional, or even municipal suffrage, although in some of the old thirteen it could have been done by an act of the legislature, a constitutional amendment not being needed. These are some of the figures for the past few years :

In Vermont, in 1892, the House passed a municipal suffrage bill—yeas 149, nays 83. In 1894 the House defeated a similar bill by a vote of 108 to 106, and refused reconsideration by a vote of 124 to 96. Thus a favorable majority of 66 in 1892 was changed to an adverse majority of 28 in 1894.

In Massachusetts, in 1894, the House passed a municipal suffrage bill by a vote of 119 to 107. In 1895 it defeated a similar bill, the vote standing, yeas 97, nays 137, on the question of carrying the bill to a third reading. In the same year an act was passed permitting all persons qualified to vote for school committee to express their opinion at the state election by voting " Yes " or " No," to the question : " Is it expedient that municipal suffrage be granted to women ? " Not one woman in four voted in favor of the proposition, although if suffrage has any traditionary power outside of New York State, that power should have been felt in Massachusetts.

In Maine, in 1893, the Senate passed a municipal suffrage bill, which was defeated in the House. In 1895 the House passed a municipal suffrage bill, which was defeated in the Senate.

In New Hampshire, in 1895, the House refused a third reading to a municipal suffrage bill, by a vote of 185 to 108.

In Connecticut, in 1895, the Senate rejected a House municipal suffrage bill, while a presidential suffrage bill did not reach a vote. And in Rhode Island a proposition for a suffrage Constitutional amendment was referred to the next legislature.

All these States had granted school suffrage and could grant municipal suffrage by act of the legislature. In 1893 municipal suffrage bills were defeated in Minnesota, Missouri, North

Dakota, and South Dakota. Full suffrage bills were defeated in Arizona and New Mexico. A township suffrage bill was defeated in Illinois, a license suffrage bill in Connecticut, and a village suffrage bill in New York. In that year, also, the Supreme Courts gave decisions adverse to suffrage laws. In 1893 a bill was defeated in the United States Senate which proposed to give women the municipal vote in the Cherokee Outlet. The vote stood 40 to 9.

In Washington Territory the Legislature passed a law conferring suffrage on woman in 1883; but this was declared invalid by the courts in 1887, because its nature was not sufficiently defined in its title. It was re-enacted in 1888, and again declared invalid by the United States Territorial Court, on the ground that the Act of Congress which organized the Territorial legislature did not empower it to extend the suffrage to women. In 1889 the people, in forming their State constitution, decided against suffrage.

In 1894, in the election of November 6, Kansas defeated a constitutional amendment granting full suffrage, by a majority of 34,827.

In Iowa, in the same year, the Senate defeated a proposition to submit a suffrage constitutional amendment to the people. In 1895, bills for full suffrage and for municipal suffrage again failed to pass, and the question was submitted to the people in 1896, and resulted in defeat.

In 1895, also, a township suffrage bill was twice defeated in Illinois.

In Indiana a proposition to strike the word "male" out of the Constitution, was not even reported from the committee to which it was referred.

In the same year, in Kansas, a bill passed the Senate which proposed to confer upon nine specified women the full suffrage in response to their petition. The Senate also passed a bill conferring upon women the vote for presidential electors; but neither ever reached a vote in the House. In Michigan, the same year, a proposition to submit a constitutional amendment was defeated, and a similar resolution in Missouri was also defeated. Montana, North Dakota, South Dakota, Washington, Wisconsin, and South Carolina also defeated propositions to submit the question to the people in 1895.

Since January, 1897, Nova Scotia, two Territories, and ten States have dealt with the suffrage proposal, and all but one of these have rendered adverse decisions. In Nova Scotia an old bill was reconsidered, and a larger majority was obtained against it. The territories are Arizona and Oklahoma. The states in which it was defeated are Iowa, Nevada, Nebraska, Kansas, Delaware, Maine, Massachusetts, and California. The last two had given it heavy defeats but a few months previously. Indiana's Supreme Court handed down an adverse decision. The favorable state was Washington, where the Legislature voted to submit an amendment to the people next year.

Certainly, the question cannot be said not to have received the attention that any vital subject might have claimed, and the answers show that, as comprehension of the meaning of democracy has grown, and as liberty of thought and action for men and women has increased, the proposition to cast an unequal burden, not upon a disfranchised class, but upon an unfranchised sex which in every class has its own correlative and equal duties, rights, and privileges, is losing ground.

But, it is answered, look at the suffrage triumphs in Utah State and Idaho. Let us look at them more closely. It is my opinion that a few more such triumphs would end in its utter overthrow. Utah introduced suffrage by a simple legislative act. Woman suffrage was abolished in Utah Territory by Federal statute, because it was found to be sustaining the Mormon Church and the institution of polygamy. The Suffragists profess to hold in abhorrence churchly and polygamous rule. Here was an opportunity for them to say to the Government : "This is not what we meant by suffrage, nor what we desire suffrage to be used for. We approve this real disfranchisement." Did they do anything of the kind? Far from it. In 1876 they passed the following : "Resolved, That, the right of suffrage being vested in the women of Utah by their constitutional and lawful enfranchisement, and by six years of use, we denounce the proposition about to be again presented to Congress for the disfranchisement of the women of that Territory, as an outrage on the freedom of thousands of legal voters and a gross innovation of vested rights; we demand the abolition of the system of numbering the ballots, in order that the women may be thoroughly free to vote as they choose, without supervision or dictation; and that the chair appoint a committee of three persons, with power to add to their number, to memorialize Congress, and otherwise watch over the rights of women of Utah in this regard during the next twelvemonth."

In 1878 the report of Utah's governor contained the following: " All voters must be over twenty-one years of age, and must have resided in the Territory six months, and in the precinct one month. If males, they must be native born or naturalized citizens of the United States, and tax-payers in the Territory. A female voter need not be a tax-payer, and if the wife, widow or daughter of a native or naturalized citizen, need not herself be native or naturalized!" In 1892 the Utah Commission made to the Secretary of the Interior a report which gave it as their opinion that the sanction of the Church had been withdrawn only temporarily in regard to polygamous practices, and would be restored after a political purpose had been served. That same year a party was formed calling itself the " Lib-

eral Party," and it carried Salt Lake City in the
first election in which National party lines were
drawn.  This was one plank of its platform:
" Anxious as every Liberal is to see every difference adjusted, as anxious as they are to exercise
the utmost privileges accorded to the most favored
Americans, they remember what first caused clash-
ing here was the presence and control of an un-
yielding Theocracy and an *imperium in imperio*,
and they cannot fail to note that at the last con-
ference of this theocratic organization the old
assumptions were all renewed."   They therefore
deprecated immediate Statehood.   The bill granting it passed Congress in 1894.   The Republican,
Democratic and Populist parties in Utah all
favored Statehood, and at the election following
the Constitutional Convention these parties all
inserted planks favoring free coinage of silver
16 to 1, demanding the return by government of
"real estate belonging to the Mormon Church,"
and favoring the retention of woman suffrage.

The women of Utah were greatly in evidence
during the late presidential election.   Several of
them were candidates for office; but it is a significant fact that, even in Utah, and even on the
Republico-Demo-Populist ticket, the women's vote
ran far behind that for the men.   " The Salt Lake
Herald " for November 13, 1896, records the fact
that " Woman suffrage gave Utah to Bryan," and
in another place it says: " The women on both
tickets polled a small number of votes."   Martha

Cannon, who was elected State Senator, obtained 8,167 votes. The men on the same ticket, elected to the same office, polled, respectively, 9,875, 9,355, 9,244, 9,036 votes. Mrs. Cannon was on the free silver ticket against her husband, who was nominated for the same office on the Republican ticket. Of the other candidates for the senatorships on that ticket, four were men and one a woman. The men's vote stood: 6,405, 6,197, 6,129, 5,961. The woman's was 4,692. The only woman put up for State Representative ran 2,000 votes behind her ticket. One man only, "the ex-dog-catcher" of the county, fell below her. The woman's vote was 4,879, the dog-catcher's 4,325.

I copy from the "Salt Lake Herald" a few sentences taken from an interview with Mrs. Cannon, State Senator elect. When asked if she was a strong believer in woman suffrage, she answered: "Of course I am. It will help women, and it will purify politics. Women are better than men. Slaves are always better than their masters." "Do you refer to polygamy?" was asked. "Indeed I do not," she answered. "I believe in polygamy. My father and mother were Mormons, and I am a Mormon. . . . A plural wife isn't half as much of a slave as a single wife. If her husband has four wives, she has three weeks of freedom every single month. . . . Of course it is all at an end now, but I think the women of Utah think, with me, that we were better off in polygamy. . . . Sixty per cent. of the voters of this State are women. We control the State. . . . What am I going to do with my children while I am making the laws for the State? The same thing I have done with them when I have been practicing medicine. They have been left to themselves a good deal. . . . Some day there will be a law compelling people to have no more than a certain amount of children, and the mothers of the land can live as they ought to live." This is the character and opinion presented by the highest State official that woman suffrage has as yet given to the United States. Comment upon it seems unnecessary, so far as it would be needed to express the disgust of the majority of American women at such sentiments and such a situation. But has any Suffrage speaker or meeting denounced them, or deprecated the result of the election? I have heard of none. The National Suffrage Convention, which was held in Iowa, in January, 1897, had the newly-elected Populist women as guests of honor, and held a jubilation over the two new Suffrage States —Utah and Idaho. Idaho has elected a Populist woman or two. The vote in that State in favor of the gold standard and that against woman suffrage tally within forty-two votes.

The instinctive alliance of the Woman Suffrage movement with the uncertain and dangerous elements in our political life is well exemplified by the campaign in California in connection with the late presidential election. Mrs. Barclay Hazard, who was almost the sole woman to express publicly the opposition which the majority of women felt, to the Suffrage idea, has given me the following clear account of the conditions and result. She says: "If the advocates of Woman Suffrage give a really frank and truthful answer to the question, 'What caused the defeat of the movement in the late campaign in California?' they must reply, 'Public sentiment was against it.' In all fairness, there is no other reason. Let us consider the conditions under which the campaign was carried on. In the first place, the Suffragists were most fortunate in choosing a time when the whole country, as well as the State of California, was torn by a question of such vital importance to continued life and well-being that all other matters were in danger of going by default.

"Second: They were extremely well organized and had command of a campaign fund of no mean magnitude, which enabled them to keep in the field such able and experienced agitators as Miss Susan B. Anthony and the Rev. Anna Shaw, to say nothing of numerous lesser lights.

"Third: There was absolutely no organized opposition to the movement. The women who disapproved were as a rule entirely unaccustomed to public speaking and were averse to coming forward in any way. They remonstrated in private but would not express their views openly.

"Fourth: Last but by no means least, our Suf-

7

frage friends may be said to have had the press
of the State with them.    The 'Los Angeles
Times' (the most influential paper in the southern part of the State) cannot be said to have aided
the movement, neither did it actively antagonize
it beyond admitting to its columns occasionally
letters from the 'Antis.'   Yet for this small opposition I heard an ardent advocate propose that
the Suffragists should boycott the paper!

"Now, was ever a cause fought for under
conditions more conducive to success?  'Every
thing,' to use a current slang phrase, 'seemed to
be going their way.'   They fully expected to win,
and those of us most opposed to their ideas in
private sadly conceded their probable victory.
The result when it came was all the more a surprise and blow to the Suffragists and a welcome
reassurance to the friends of stability and con-
servatism.    The figures show us that while the
stronghold of Populism, the South, went for the
measure, Alameda County turned the scale.   One
must know California to realize what that means.
Alameda County contains the city of Oakland,
which is admittedly the most respectable and
moral city in California; it also contains the
town of Berkeley, which is the home of the University of California with its large faculty of
clever men, most of them from the East.    Yes, it
was here in the stronghold of morals and intellect
that the Woman Suffrage movement in California met its fate."

A question constantly and properly asked is: "How does woman suffrage work where it is exercised?" So far as I can obtain information, where it has worked at all, it has been detrimental to women and to the State.

Of Wyoming there is much testimony to the fact that during the Territorial period (1868–'89) women did little voting, and played no appreciable part in political life. Populism and Free Coinage had begun to play a prominent part in the whole section when Wyoming was admitted to Statehood in 1890. At the election that followed its admission there was a fusion that resulted in the election of a Populist Governor, and such was the riotous state of feeling that the Governor was obliged to enter the State House through a broken window. A year later this same Governor, in his annual message, proclaimed woman suffrage to be a notable success. As a proof, he pointed to the fact that there were no criminals in the State, and that the jails were empty. A little research into official documents showed that there might be other reasons, because the criminals and those guilty of small offences were at that time lodged in other States, and a year later, when the authorities took possession of Laramie Prison, given by the Government, and brought home their evil-doers, they outnumbered, in proportion to population, those of New Mexico, which certainly should be a fair place for comparison.

For a time, women served on juries, and there

is testimony to the fact that in many respects they
served well. But the practice of calling them was
soon suspended, and never has been renewed.
The only public office of consequence held by
them was bestowed by the Republicans but a year
or two ago, when Miss Reel was made State Superintendent of Schools. In our late crucial election, Wyoming and its woman suffrage gave their
voices for Populism and Free Coinage. The
scale hung in the balance. Why, if woman is a
greater political power for good than man, did
she not turn it for the principles which the State
had held were best? The true test of the working of woman suffrage lies in a study of the legislation connected with it, and this will be presented under its appropriate heading.

The scenes of shameful defiance of law and
order in the midst of which Colorado admitted
woman to the ballot are of more recent occurrence
and are fresh in memory. Populism never has
played in Colorado the part that it has in Kansas, but "anything for free coinage" has been
the motto, and in abiding by it the State brought
in, and afterward turned out, Gov. Waite, of disgraceful memory. Again, last year, there was
Republican-Democratic-Populist fusion to beat
the gold standard, and much Populist rule was
again the result. One good authority writes
me that women "have introduced an element of
order and respectability upon election day that
was never observed before." He says he thinks

that, "as a whole, the people are very much satisfied with woman suffrage and believe that it
has resulted beneficially in so far as it has made
politics a little better than they were." Another
says that "the influence of woman in politics did
not prevent the last Republican caucus of Arapa-
hoe Co. from being the most disgraceful in the
history of the State. The Convention, though
presided over by a woman, was completely in the
power of the 'gang,' and sent to Pueblo the most
unworthy delegate ever sent." This gentleman
also says he has "heard numbers of intelligent
women state that they were sorry the ballot had
ever been given to them." Orderliness at the ordinary elections is expected here, without calling
upon women to act as "moral police" at the polls.
So quiet are they that it has been found practicable to place coffee-stands in charge of women
near some of the booths, when women have re-
quested it in the hope of preventing drunkenness.
A friend said to me some time ago: "You know
that I have been a Suffragist. I am most thoroughly converted. I have been three months in
Colorado. It is enough to cure any one."

A Denver correspondent of the "Chicago
Record," says: "The women of Colorado took no
active part in the recent campaign, but they did
not forget to vote. . . . The experiment of having
women in the State Assembly did not prove satisfactory, at the last session, and it was quite generally
conceded that there would be no more women

sent to that body; but the Populists won in this county, and on their ticket were three woman candidates, so the coming session will again have three women as members."

Of course the effect of suffrage in new States is not a criterion of its effect elsewhere. And whether the effect could be shown to be good or bad, the main argument would not be touched. The interesting thing to trace is the affiliations of the movement.

In addition to those that have been mentioned we recall the fact that in our recent political campaign, four parties that nominated candidates for President and Vice-President of the United States, had in their conventions women as delegates and members of committees. They were the Populist, the Free-Silver, the Prohibition, and the Socialist-Labor parties. The woman-suffragists of the Prohibition party left the rock-ribbed champion that had put a Suffrage plank in every platform for years, in order to go with Free Silver and Populism of the most extravagant type. These parties also had Suffrage planks. Altgeld and Debs, Coxey and Tillman were only men, but Mary Ellen Lease furnished to the campaign that strain of exalted fanaticism that at once points out woman's glory and woman's danger.

The Suffrage indictment we have been considering is summed up as follows: " Now, in view of this entire disfranchisement of one half of the people of this country, their social and religious degradation—in view of the unjust laws above mentioned, and because women do feel themselves aggrieved, oppressed, and fraudulently deprived of their most sacred rights, we insist that they have immediate admission to all the rights and privileges which belong to them as citizens of the United States."

Dr. Jacobi in "Common Sense" says: "To this very day the survivors of that group of pioneer women have an abstract way of stating their claim which, to modern ears, sounds somewhat archaic."

She is not archaic when she says: "During the long ages of class rule, which are just beginning to cease, only one form of sovereignty has been assigned to all men—that, namely, over all women. Upon these feeble and inferior companions all men were permitted to avenge the indignities they suffered from so many men to whom they were forced to submit."

Mary A. Livermore is not archaic when in the "North American Review" for February, 1896, she says: "Her physical weakness, and not alone her mental inferiority, has made her the subject of man. Toiling patiently for him, cheerfully sharing with him all his perils and hardships, the unappreciated mother of his children, she has been bought and sold, petted and tortured, according to the whims of her brutal owner, the victim everywhere of pillage, lust, war, and servitude. And this statement includes all races and peoples of the earth from the date of their historic existence." .

I deny the truthfulness of the archaic accusation, and denounce as an absurdity the bombastic demand. I resent, as an unwarranted insult to woman and to man, the still more bitter modern representations of woman's condition and woman's rights in this world, and especially in this Republic. They are simply false.

Archaic or modern, the dictums of the Suffrage pioneers have been repeated at their every convention. Overlaid with sentiment as much of the Suffrage idea has become, contradictory as it is in argument and in statement of fact, blended as are its sophisms with the real progress of the time, sincere and well-meaning as are many of its advocates, sex antagonism is the corner-stone of its foundation. The Woman's Rebellion is a more complex affair than the American Revolution. The latter was the natural result of the earnest and united protest, by a large majority of men and women of the American Colonies, against the tyranny of a monarchical government. The former was a protest by a small band of women and men against what they claimed to be universal tyranny. They attacked law and custom all along the line, and the weapon forever kept in order for the service was the demand for woman's possession of the ballot. Where she does not possess it, and has not asked it, her influence is mightiest. The relation of woman to the Republic

is a study worthy the most exalted patriotism.
In it is involved the broader question· of her re-
lation to man and to the destiny of the race.
When told of her son's heroism in crossing the
Delaware, Mary Washington said, "George will
not forget the lessons I have taught him."
Through the mother's devoted faith and the son's
obedient power, the foundations were laid of a
government whose sole reliance must still be on
woman's inspiration and man's willing strength.
These are evidently God's instruments for our
Nation's upbuilding.

# CHAPTER IV.

The extinction of human bondage, more perhaps than any other one event, has emphasized the progress of the century about to close. Our generation has witnessed the destruction of serfdom in Russia, and of slavery in Brazil and the United States. Freedom was gained; but of the enlightened rulers through whom it was won, two were assassinated and one was exiled to die. Sacrifice is still the price of liberty.

Much stress has been laid by Suffragists upon the supposed fact that the Woman-suffrage movement grew up as a logical conclusion from the Anti-slavery movement. It grew out of it in the sense of having been born in its midst; but I believe that the truth will be found to be that it was the most prolific source of the dissensions that marred that noble cause, and was identified with the small element that adopted wild notions or used the notoriety gained by opposition to slavery in order to propagate mischief. The conduct of those who later entered the Suffrage movement hindered the public work of women from the time of organized effort for the slave until slavery fell pierced to death amid the horrors of a fratricidal war. I will take a brief survey of the Anti-slavery struggle as it blended itself with the doctrines of those abolitionists who were the earliest and staunchest friends of the Suffrage movement, and compare it with the statements and claims of the women themselves.

I first refer to the " Life of James G. Birney," by his son, General William Birney. James G. Birney was an early friend of Henry B. Stanton, husband of Elizabeth Cady Stanton, and with him helped to lay the foundations of the Free-Soil Party, and later the Republican Party. General Birney says of his father : " In his visit to New York and New England, in May and June, 1837, Mr. Birney's chief object had been to restore harmony among Anti-slavery leaders on doctrines and measures, and especially to check a tendency, already marked in Massachusetts, to burden the cause with irrelevant reforms, real or supposed. With this view he had attended the New England Anti-slavery Convention held at Boston, May 30 to June 2 inclusive, accepted the position of one of its vice-presidents, and acted as a member of its committee on business. Rev. Henry C. Wright, the leader of the No-Human-Government, Woman's-Rights, and Moral-Reform factions, was a member of the Convention, but received no appointment on any committee. On June 23, in the ' Liberator ' [his newspaper], Mr. Garrison denounced human governments. July 4, he spoke

at Providence, as if approvingly, of the overthrow of the Nation, the dismemberment of the
Union, and the dashing in pieces of the Church.
July 15, an association of Congregational ministers
issued a 'pastoral letter' against the new doctrines.
August 2, five clergymen, claiming to represent
nine tenths of the abolitionists of Massachusetts,
published an 'appeal' which was directed more
especially against the course of the 'Liberator.'
August 3, the abolitionists of Andover Theological Seminary issued a similar appeal. Among
the complaints were some against 'speculations
that lead inevitably to disorganization, anarchy,
unsettling the domestic economy, removing the
landmarks of society, and unhinging the machinery of government.' A new Anti-slavery society
in Bangor passed the following resolution : 'That,
while we admit the right of full and free discussion of all subjects, yet, in our judgment, individuals rejecting the authority of civil and pa-
rental governments ought not to be employed as
agents and lecturers in promoting the cause of
emancipation.'"

In his Autobiography, speaking of this time,
Frederick Douglass says: "I believe my first
offence against our Anti-slavery Israel was committed during these Syracuse meetings. It was
in this wise : Our general agent, John A. Collins,
had recently returned from England full of communistic ideas, which ideas would do away with
individual property and have all things in com-

mon. He had arranged a corps of speakers of his communistic persuasion, consisting of John O. Wattles, Nathaniel Whiting, and John Orvis, to follow our Anti-slavery conventions, and while our meeting was in progress in Syracuse Mr. Collins came in with his new friends and doctrines and proposed to adjourn our Anti-slavery discussions and take up the subject of communism. To this I ventured to object. I held that it was imposing an additional burden of unpopularity on our cause, and an act of bad faith with the people who paid the salary of Mr. Collins and were responsible for these hundred conventions. Strange to say, my course in this matter did not meet the approval of Mrs. Maria W. Chapman, an influential member of the board of managers of the Massachusetts Anti-slavery society, and called out a sharp reprimand from her, for insubordination to my superiors." John O. Wattles labored hard to introduce Woman Suffrage into the State Constitution of Kansas. Mr. Collins worked for it in California in the early days. Mrs. Chapman, who had embraced Mr. Collins's doctrines, was one of the first pillars of the Suffrage movement.

Later, when Mr. Douglass determined to establish a newspaper and become its editor, he was obliged to leave New England, "for the sake of peace," he says, as his Anti-slavery friends opposed it, saying that it was absurd to think of a wood-sawyer offering himself as an editor. In Rochester, N. Y., he established "The North

Star." He says, "I was then a faithful disciple of William L. Garrison, and fully committed to his doctrine touching the pro-slavery character of the Constitution of the United States, also the non-voting principle, of which he was the known and distinguished advocate. With him, I held it to be the first duty of the non-slaveholding States to dissolve the union with the slaveholding States, and hence my cry, like his, was ' No union with slaveholders.' After a time, a careful reconsideration of the subject convinced me that there was no necessity for ' dissolving the union between the northern and southern States;' that to seek this dissolution was no part of my duty as an abolitionist; that to abstain from voting was to refuse to exercise a legitimate and powerful means for abolishing slavery ; and that the Constitution of the United States not only contained no guarantees in favor of slavery, but, on the contrary, was in its letter and spirit an Anti-slavery instrument, demanding the abolition of slavery as a condition of its own existence as the supreme law of the land. This radical change in my opinions produced a corresponding change in my action. Those who could not see any honest reasons for changing their views, as I had done, could not easily see any such reasons for my change, and the common punishment of apostates was mine. . . . Among friends who had been devoted to my cause were Isaac and Amy Post, William and Mary Hallowell, Asa and Hulda Anthony, and indeed all the committee of the Western New York Anti-Slavery Society. They held festivals and fairs to raise money, and assisted me in every other possible way to keep my paper in circulation while I was a non-voting abolitionist, but withdrew from me when I became a voting abolitionist."

The Posts, the Hallowells, and the Anthonys were among the first to attach themselves to the Suffrage movement.

The Grimké sisters, who were intensely interested in the abolition agitation, followed Garrison to the extreme, and adopted the socialistic ideas with which his wing became to a large extent identified. They were also early in the Suffrage cause. In August, 1837, Whittier wrote to them as follows: "I am anxious to hold a long conversation with you on the subject of war, human government, and church and family government. The more I reflect upon the subject the more difficulty I find, and the more decidedly am I of opinion that we ought to hold all these matters aloof from the cause of abolition. Our good friend, H. C. Wright, with the best intentions in the world, is doing great injury by a different course. He is making the Anti-slavery party responsible in a great degree for his, to say the least, startling opinions. . . . But let him keep them distinct from the cause of emancipation. To employ an agent who devotes half his time and talents to the propagation of ' no-human or no-family government' doctrines in connection, *intimate* connection, with the doctrines of abolition, is a fraud upon the patrons of the cause. Brother Garrison errs, I think, in this respect. He takes the 'no-church and no-government' ground."

Mr. Garrison wrote to the American Anti-slavery Society of his desire to crush the "dissenters," and Maria W. Chapman wrote: "Why will they think they can cut away from Garrison without becoming an abomination? . . . If this defection should drink the cup and end all, we of Massachusetts will turn and abolish them as readily as we would the colonization society." Henry B. Stanton wrote to William Goodell: "I am glad to see that you have criticised Brother H. C. Wright. I have just returned from a few months' tour in eastern Massachusetts, and he has done immense hurt there." A. A. Phelps, agent of the Massachusetts Anti-Slavery society, wrote: "I write you this in great grief, and yet I feel constrained to do it. The cause of abolition here was never in so dangerous and critical a position before. Mutual jealousies on the part of the laity and clergy are rampant; indeed, so much so that, let a clerical brother do what he will, it is resolved as a matter of course into a sinister motive! . . . Of this stamp, more than ever before, is friend Garrison. And Mrs. Chapman remarked to me the other day that she sometimes doubted which needed abolition most, slavery or the black-hearted ministry. For this cause alone we are on the brink of a general split in our ranks. . . . And as if to make a bad matter worse, Garrison insists on yoking perfectionism, no-governmentism, and woman-preaching with abolition, as part and parcel of the same lump."

In 1840, Emerson, in his Amory Hall lecture, said : " The Church or religious party is falling from the Church nominal, and is appearing in Temperance and non-resistant societies, in movements of abolitionists and socialists, and in very significant assemblies called Sabbath and Bible conventions, composed of ultraists, of seekers, of all the soul and soldiery of dissent, and meeting to call in question the authority of the Sabbath, of the priesthood, of the Church. In these movements nothing was more remarkable than the discontent they begot in the movers. . . . They defied each other like a congress of kings, each of whom had a realm to rule, and a way of his own that made concert unprofitable."

These ideas blossomed, in due course of time, into Socialistic communities. There was a distinctly Anti-slavery one at Hopedale, Massachusetts. The founder, Adin Ballou, published a tract setting forth the objects of the community, from which I make the following extracts : " No precise theological dogmas, ordinances, or ceremonies are prescribed or prohibited. In such matters all the members are free, with mutual love and toleration, to follow their own highest

8

convictions of truth and religious duty, answerable only to the great Head of the Church Universal. It enjoins total abstinence from all God-contemning words and deeds; all unchastity; all intoxicating beverages; all oath-taking; all slaveholding and pro-slavery compromises; all war and preparations for war; all capital and other vindictive punishments; all insurrectionary, seditious, mobocratic, and personal violence against any government, society, family, or individual; all voluntary participation in any anti-Christian government, under promise of unqualified support, whether by doing military service, commencing actions at law, holding office, voting, petitioning for penal laws, or asking public interference for protection which can only be given by such force. It is the seedling of the true democratic and social Republic, wherein neither caste, color, sex, nor age stands prescribed. It is a moral-suasion temperance society on the teetotal basis. It is a moral-power Anti-slavery society, radical and without compromise. It is a peace society on the only impregnable foundation, that of Christian non-resistance. It is a sound theoretical and practical Woman's Rights Association." Among other Suffragists, Abby Kelly Foster was resident at Hopedale. Another community, at Northampton, was sometimes described as " Nothingarian."

Of the state of things at this time in the Anti-slavery societies, General Birney says, " The no-government men made up in activity what they

lacked in numbers. While refusing for them-
·selves to vote at the ballot-box, they voted in
conventions and formed coalitions with women
who wished to vote at the ballot-box." Mr.
Henry B. Stanton wrote to William Goodell:
" An effort was made at the annual meeting of
the Massachusetts society, which adjourned to-
day, to make its annual report and its action
subservient to the non-resistant movement, and
through the votes of the women of Lynn and
Boston it succeeded." A little later, January,
1839, Mr. Stanton wrote again to Mr. Goodell, as
follows: "I have taken the liberty to show your
letter to brothers Phelps, George Allen, George
Russell, O. Scott, N. Colver, and a large number
of others, and they highly approve its sentiments.
They, with you, are fully of the opinion that it is
high time to take a firm stand against the no-
government doctrine. They are far from regarding it merely as a humbug." John A. Collins, the
Anti-slavery agent referred to, founded a community at Skaneateles, N. Y., based upon the
following dictums: A disbelief in any special revelation of God to Man, in any form of worship,
in any special regard for the Sabbath, in any
church, disbelief in all governments based on physical force, because they are " organized bands of
banditti," whose authority is to be disregarded,
a disbelief in voting, in petitioning, in doing military duty, paying personal or property taxes,
serving on juries, testifying in " so-called " courts

of justice. A disbelief in any individual property. A belief that as marriage is designed for the happiness of the parties to it, when such parties have outlived their affections, the sooner the separation takes place the better, and that such separation shall not be a barrier to their again uniting with any one. The community lived two and a half years, and broke up with a debt of ten thousand dollars. John O. Wattles, who was associated with Collins in the disturbance referred to by Frederick Douglass, founded a community in Logan County, Ohio, which was called "The Prairie Home." They had no laws, no government, no opinions, no principles, no form of society, no test of admission. They professed to take for their creed the dictum "Do as you would be done by." The association broke up in anarchy within a few months. Mr. Collins and Mr. Wattles were always promoters of the Woman-Suffrage movement.

Mr. Garrison said : " We cannot acknowledge allegiance to any human government. We can allow no appeal to patriotism to revenge any national insult or injury." Again he said : "If a nation has no right to defend itself against foreign enemies, no individual possesses that right in his own case. . . . As every human government is upheld by physical strength, and its laws are enforced at the point of the bayonet, we cannot hold office. We therefore exclude ourselves from every legislative and judicial body, and repudiate

all human politics, worldly honors, and stations
of authority."

Ralph Waldo Emerson says: "They withdraw
themselves from the common labors and competi-
tions of the market and the caucus. . . . They
are striking work, and calling out for something
worthy to do. . . . They are not good citizens,
not good members of society; unwilling to bear
their part of the public burdens. They do not
even like to vote. They filled the world with
long beards and long words. They began in
words, and ended in words."

Charles Sumner said: "An omnibus-load of
Boston abolitionists has done more harm to the
Anti-slavery cause than all its enemies."

Angelina Grimké, writing at this time to Mr.
Weld, said: "What wouldst thou think of the
'Liberator' abandoning abolitionism as a primary
object, and becoming the vehicle of all these
grand principles?"

In his published volume "Anti-slavery Days,"
James Freeman Clarke says of the first Garrison
Anti-slavery society: "There was no such excitement to be had anywhere else as at these meetings.
There was a little of everything going on in them.
Sometimes crazy people would come in and insist
on taking up the time; sometimes mobs would
interrupt the smooth tenor of their way; but amid
all disturbance each meeting gave us an interesting and impressive hour. I think that some of
the Garrisonian orators had the keenest tongues

ever given to man.   Stephen S. Foster and Henry
C. Wright, for example, said the sharpest things
that were ever uttered.   Their belief was, that
people were asleep, and the only thing to be done
was to rouse them ; and to do this it was necessary to cut deep and spare not.   The more angry
people were made, the better." Again, in the
same volume, he says, after describing the political Anti-slavery party :   " While these political
anti-slavery movements were going on, the old
abolitionists, under the lead of Garrison, Phillips,
and others, had decided to oppose all voting
and all political efforts under the Constitution.
They adopted as their motto, 'No union with
slaveholders.'   Their hope for abolishing slavery
was in inducing the North to dissolve the Union.
Edmund Quincy said the Union was 'a confed-
eracy with crime,' that ' the experiment of a
great nation with popular institutions had sig-
nally failed,' that ' the Republic was not a model
but a warning to the nations ;' that ' the whole
people must be either slaveholders or slaves;'
that the only escape for ' the slave from his bondage was over the ruins of the American Church
and the American State:' and it was the unalter-
able purpose of the Garrisonians to labor for the
dissolution of the Union."   Freeman Clarke goes
on to say: " Wendell Phillips said on one occasion, ' Thank God, I am not a citizen of the United
States.'   As late as 1861 he declared the Union
a failure, and argued for the dissolution of the

Union as 'the best possible method of abolishing slavery.' If the North had agreed to disunion and had followed the advice of Phillips, 'To build a bridge of gold to take the slave States out of the Union,' slavery would probably be still existing in all the Southern States. At all events, it was not abolished by those who wished for disunion, but by those who were determined at all hazards and by every sacrifice to maintain the Union."

On April 8, 1839, Henry B. Stanton wrote to William Goodell as follows: "At this very time, and mainly, too, in that part of the country where political action has been most successful, and whence, from its promise of soon being triumphant, great encouragement was derived by abolitionists everywhere, a sect has arisen in our midst whose members regard it as of religious obligation in no case to exercise the elective franchise. This persuasion is part and parcel of the tenet which it is believed they have embraced, that as Christians have the precepts of the gospel of Christ, and the spirit of God to guide them, all human governments, as necessarily including the idea of force to secure obedience, are not only superfluous, but unlawful encroachments on the Divine government as ascertained from the sources above mentioned. Therefore they refuse to do anything voluntarily that would be considered as acknowledging the lawful existence of human governments. Denying to civil governments the right to use force, they easily deduce that family governments have no such right. They carry out the 'non-resistant' theory. To the first ruffian who would demand our purse or oust us from our house, they are to be unconditionally surrendered unless moral suasion be found sufficient to induce him to desist from his purpose. Our wives, our daughters, our sisters, our mothers, we are to see set upon by the most brutal, without any effort on our part except argument to defend them! And even they themselves are forbidden to use in defence of their purity such powers as God has endowed them with for its protection, if resistance should be attended with injury or destruction to the assailant. In short, the 'no-government' doctrines, as they are believed now to be embraced, seem to strike at the root of the social structure, and tend, so far as I am able to judge of their tendency, to throw society into entire confusion and to renew, under the sanction of religion, scenes of anarchy and license that have generally hitherto been the offspring of the rankest infidelity and irreligion.'"

Again, he wrote: "The non-government doctrine, stripped of its disguise, is worse than Fanny-Wrightism, and, under a Gospel garb, it is Fanny-Wrightism with a white frock on. It goes to the utter overthrow of all order, yea, of all purity. When carried out, it goes not only for a community of goods, but a community of wives. Strange that such an infidel theory should find votaries in New England!"

The editors of the "History of Woman Suf-

frage" say in their opening chapter: " Among
the immediate causes that led to the demand for
the equal political rights of women, in this country, we may note these: First, the discussion in
several of the State legislatures of the property
rights of married women; Second, the great educational work that was accomplished by the able
lectures of Frances Wright, on political, religious,
and social questions.  Ernestine L. Rose, following in her wake, equally liberal in her religious
opinions, and equally well-informed on the science
of government, helped to deepen and perpetuate
the impression Frances Wright had made on the
minds of unprejudiced hearers.  Third, and above
all other causes of the Woman-Suffrage movement,
was the Anti-slavery struggle in this country."
By referring to the columns of the secular and
religious press of that period, we find that most of
the respectable and representative opinion of the
country was "prejudiced."  Halls and assembly
rooms in all the cities were closed against Fanny
Wright, not only because her doctrines were
absolutely infidel and materialistic, but because
they were deemed subversive of law, order, and
decency.  The better portion of society in the
United States was of one mind in its estimate of
" The Pioneer Woman in the Cause of Woman's
Rights," as she was called.  In the columns of
" The Free Inquirer," a newspaper which she and
Robert Dale Owen established and edited in New
York City in 1829, she attacked religion in every

form, marriage, the family, and the State. She
pretended to no basis of scientific investigation,
but in a brilliant flood of words endeavored to
sweep away faith in the Bible, the home, the Republic, in favor of negation, communism, free love.
I have place for but a single quotation from one
of her " Fables," published in the " Free Inquirer." It will show the drift of her work in one
direction :

" ' Is my errand sped, and am I a master on
earth ? ' said the infernal king (Pluto). ' Even as
I promised,' said the Fury. ' Love hath forsaken
the earth. Under the form of religion I aroused
the fears and commanded the submission of mor-
tals ; and our imp now reigns on earth in the place
of Love, under the form of Hymen.' Pluto smiled
grimly, and smote his thigh in triumph. ' Well
conceited, well executed, daughter of Night. Our
empire shall not lack recruits, now that innocence
is exchanged for superstition, and the true affection of congenial and confiding hearts is replaced
by mock ceremonies and compulsory oaths ! ' "

Frances Wright had founded, in 1825, at Na-
shoba, Tennessee, a community that had for its
professed aim the elevation and education of the
Southern negroes. In describing her object, Miss
Wright said : " No difference will be made in the
schools between the white children and the children of color, whether in education or in any other
advantage. This establishment is founded on the
principle of community of property and labor :

these fellow-creatures, that is, the blacks, admitted here, requiting these services by services equal or greater, by filling occupations which their habits render easy, and which to their guides and assistants might be difficult or unpleasing." This form of helotism flourished but three years on American soil. It is doubly interesting as containing the germs of communism and anti-slavery that blended themselves in the beginnings of a movement for suffrage which was directly inspired by Frances Wright.

The editors of the "Suffrage History" say that "above all other causes of the suffrage movement, was the Anti-slavery struggle in this country." They add: "In the early Anti-slavery conventions, the broad principles of human rights were so exhaustively discussed, justice, liberty, and equality so clearly taught, that the women who crowded to listen, readily learned the lesson of freedom for themselves, and early began to take part in the debates and business affairs of all associations. And before the public were aroused to the dangerous innovation, women were speaking in crowded promiscuous assemblies. The clergy opposed to the Abolition movement first took alarm, and issued a pastoral letter, warning their congregations against the influence of such women. The clergy identified with Anti-slavery associations took alarm also, and the initiative steps to silence women, and to deprive them of the right to vote in the business meetings, were

soon taken.  This action culminated in a division
in the Anti-slavery Association.  The question of
woman's right to speak, vote, and serve on committee, not only precipitated the division in the
ranks of the American Anti-slavery society, in
1840, but it disturbed the peace of the World's
Anti-slavery Convention, held that same year in
London.  In summoning the friends of the slave
from all parts of the two hemispheres to meet in
London, John Bull never dreamed that woman,
too, would answer to his call.  Imagine, then, the
commotion in the conservative Anti-slavery circles in England when it was known that half a
dozen of those terrible women who had spoken to
promiscuous assemblies, voted on men and measures, prayed and petitioned against slavery, women
who had been mobbed, ridiculed by the press, and
denounced by the pulpit, who had been the cause
of setting all the American Abolitionists by the
ears, and split their ranks asunder, were on their
way to England."

These quarrels, stirred up through the unseemly conduct of men and women, as we have
seen, they were willing to precipitate upon a convention in a foreign land, a convention, too,
which had declared its desire not to receive them
as delegates.  Upon the calling of the roll, the
meeting was thrown into excitement and confusion
on a subject foreign to that which brought them
together.  Wendell Phillips eloquently pleaded
for the admission of the women.  The English

officers, while showing their personal courtesy, begged to remind them that the Queen, and many ladies in various stations, were represented by male delegates, and that to admit the American ladies would be to cast a slight upon their own active members, many of whom were present. During the heated discussion Mr. James Fuller said : " One friend has stated that this question should have been settled on the other side of the Atlantic. Why, it *was* so settled, and in favor of the women." Mr. James G. Birney answered : " The right of the women to sit and act in all respects as men in our Anti-slavery associations was so decided in the Society in May, 1839, but not by a large majority, which majority was swelled by the votes of the women themselves. I have just received a letter from a gentleman in New York (Lewis Tappan) communicating the fact that the persistence of the friends of promiscuous female representation in pressing that practice on the American Anti-Slavery society, at its annual meeting on the 12th of last month, had caused such disagreement that he, and others who viewed the subject as he did, were deliberating the question of seceding from the old organization."

Lewis Tappan, a founder of the American Missionary Society, was intimately connected with his brother Arthur in all anti-slavery work. Arthur was a founder of the American Tract Society, and of Oberlin College, and a benefactor of Lane Seminary. He established " The Emancipator," and was president of the American Anti-Slavery Society until compelled, with his brother Lewis, to withdraw on account of the conduct of the no-government men and women, and take nearly all the Society with him.

When the vote was taken in the London meeting the women were excluded on the ground that "it being contrary to English usage, it would subject them to ridicule and prejudice their cause."

George Thompson then said: "I hope, as this question is now decided, that Mr. Phillips will give us the assurance that we shall proceed with one heart and one mind." Mr. Phillips replied, "I have no doubt of it. There is no unpleasant feeling on our part. All we asked was an expression of opinion; we shall now act with the utmost cordiality."

But Mr. Phillips had reckoned without his host and hostesses. Mr. Garrison had not been present at the discussion, but he arrived at this juncture and took his seat with the excluded delegates. During a twelve-days' discussion of the momentous cause that had called them together, which he had professed especially to champion, he took not the slightest part. Such was his mistaken zeal that he was willing so to stultify himself, and the women were willing to applaud him in so doing. The spirit that looked upon the American Constitution as "a covenant with death and an agreement with hell" was there.

The spirit that defied all authority and could confound liberty of conscience with the formal acts of courtesy between man and man, was there. The spirit that took for its motto "You cannot shut up discord" was there. And out of these combined ˙ elements, trained in the school of thought that had treated as tyranny the religious and civil liberty of the United States, grew directly the Woman-Suffrage movement. Elizabeth Cady Stanton was not a delegate. The delegates were Abby Kelly, Esther Moore, and Lucretia Mott. Mrs. Stanton was a bride, and in the immediate party on this, their wedding trip, was Mr. Birney, her husband's special friend. The writers of the "History" say: "As the ladies were not allowed to speak in the Convention, they kept up a brisk fire, morning, noon, and night, on the unfortunate gentlemen who were domiciled at the same house." Mrs. Stanton had not been identified with any of these abolition quarrels; but she records that now she took her full share of the "firing," notwithstanding her husband's "gentle nudges under the table" and Mr. Birney's ominous frowns across it. In the volume entitled "Woman's Work in America," in a contribution called "Woman in the State," written by Mrs. Mary A. Livermore, she says: "The leaders in the new [suffrage] movement, Lucretia Mott and Mrs. Stanton, with their husbands," did thus and so in originating it. Lucretia Mott's husband was with her as a silent member of the conventions, but Elizabeth Cady Stanton's husband is conspicuous for his absence from every list of officers or attendants, from the inception of the Suffrage movement until his death. He may have been in perfect sympathy with his wife; but since the names of all the men already mentioned in connection with the mad "no-civil, no-family, no-personal government" movement, do appear, and his does not, it is impossible not to challenge Mrs. Livermore's statement. The last reference to him in the "History" was as voting on the occasion of the London meeting, in favor of the women's admission to the World's Convention. No mention is made of any speech, or of reasons given. Certain it is, that while Mr. Garrison became the conspicuous standard-bearer for the Woman's Rights movement, Mr. Stanton became one of the conspicuous bearers of the standard of the Free Soil and Republican parties, which included some of Anti-slavery's staunchest friends, who were denounced by Garrison as its foes.

Thus it seems evident to me that the Woman-Suffrage movement no more grew logically out of the great discussions on human bondage which began with Washington, Jefferson, Adams, Franklin, Hamilton, and John Jay, and ended with Sumner, Seward, and Lincoln, than the communes of this country grew out of the utterances of the Fathers based on the declaration that "All men are created equal, and are endowed with certain inalienable rights, among which are life, liberty, and the pursuit of happiness."

It was among those whose mistaken zeal and wild conduct were most mischievous, that the Suffrage sentiment gathered head. Their lack of judgment in defying the opinions of their own sex, as well as of the other, their wrapt forgetfulness of proprieties, which incited mobs and proved a fine tool for the frenzy of so-called social reformers, brought contempt upon womanhood as well as upon the cause they advocated. Women, in the churches and out, were the strength of the Anti-slavery movement; but not these women. As to the notable meeting in London, had the delegates been the highest and largest minded and most cultured of their sex, and had their cause been the noblest, they and it would have been dishonored by the method of its presentation. American women of to-day would no more applaud such conduct than did those of fifty years ago. Women have won lasting public favor and place, while Suffrage has won an uneasy footing by unenviable methods.

This survey enables us to understand what otherwise would seem most strange, how the women of the Suffrage movement, in claiming the right of suffrage, ignored the duties and powers based upon and connected with it—those that formed the defence which made possible any such nation as ours. Added to the extreme Quaker doctrine of peace-at-any-price, was the fanatical

9

notion of the sinfulness of all war, all use of physical force, and a cool assumption that opinion was
law. Mrs. Maria Chapman read, at one of the
early Woman's-Rights conventions, a string of
verses that reveals the absurdity of the situation.
It was in reply to " A Clerical Appeal," issued by
the Rev. Nehemiah Adams, whose " South-Side
View of Slavery " received more Anti-slavery
attention than it deserved, for it expressed only
his own .fantastic ideas. In the " Appeal " he
maintains that women should paint in water colors
only, not in oil. Mrs. Chapman says :

" Our patriot fathers, of eloquent fame,
    Waged war against tangible forms ;
  Aye, *their* foes were men—and if ours were the same,
    We might speedily quiet their storms ;
  But, ah ! their descendants enjoy not such bliss,
  The assumptions of Britain were nothing to this.

" Could we but array all our force in the field,
    We'd teach these usurpers of power
  That their bodily safety demands they should yield,
    And in presence of womanhood cower ;
  But alas ! for our tethered and impotent state,
  Chained by notions of knighthood—we can but debate."

     *     *     *     *     *     *     *     *

" Oh ! shade of the prophet Mahomet, arise !
    Place woman again in her ' sphere,'
  And teach that her soul was not born for the skies,
    But to flutter a brief moment here.
  This doctrine of Jesus, as preached up by Paul,
  If embraced in its spirit will ruin us all."

Mention of Mrs. Chapman recalls her attitude

toward Frederick Douglass and the further fact
that he became an advocate of Suffrage. In his
"Life and Times" he says: "I could not meet
her [Mrs. Stanton's] arguments except with the
shallow plea of 'custom,' 'natural division of
duties,' 'indelicacy of woman's taking part in
politics,' 'the common talk of woman's sphere,'
and the like, all of which that able woman
brushed away by those arguments which no man
has yet successfully refuted." Mr. Douglass
might have called to mind the fact, to the recognition of which he had been so thoroughly converted, and which he set forth on page 460 of his
book, when he wrote : " I insisted that the liberties
of the American people were dependent upon the
ballot-box, the jury-box, and the cartridge-box."
He forgot that Mrs. Stanton, in defiance of those
social laws that had weight with him, was asking
to use the first, to use partially the second, and
to ignore the third, on which both of the others
depend for continuance.

The "History" is dedicated to Harriet Martineau
(among other women) as one who influenced the
starting of the Suffrage movement. Turning to
Miss Martineau's "Society in America," published
in 1837, I find the following in her account of the
Anti-slavery movement in the United States : " The
progress of the Abolition question within three
years throughout the whole of the rural districts of
the North, is a far stronger testimony to the virtue
of the nation than the noisy clamor of a portion of

the slaveholders of the South, and the merchant
aristocracy of the North, and the silence of the
clergy, against it.  The nation must not be judged
of by that portion whose worldly interests are
involved in the maintenance of the anomaly ; nor
yet by the eight hundred flourishing Abolition
societies of the North, with all the supporters
they have in unassociated individuals.  If it be
found that the five Abolitionists who first met in
a little chamber five years ago, to measure their
moral strength against this national enormity,
have become a host beneath whose assaults the
vicious institution is rocking to its foundations,
it is time that slavery was ceasing to be a national
reproach."

An observer who could be made to believe that
these five Abolitionists had really accomplished
more toward the overthrow of slavery than eight
hundred flourishing Abolition societies and their
outside supporters, and that the great body of
clergymen were silent, because they did not adopt
the methods of the five who set themselves against
church and state, shows a credulity that leads one
to question the information and the conclusions
on which her judgment of the relation of American women to the Republic were based.

As a proof that when women entered into
public work in a womanly way they found support from the church and the Abolitionists, we
may point to perhaps the first organized charitable
and industrial work done among women in this

country. In 1834 Mrs. Charles Hawkins, of New York City, had convened in the Third Free Church, corner of Houston and Thompson streets, a meeting which resulted in the immediate formation of "The Moral Reform Society." Clergymen who were in sympathy with the movement addressed the meeting. "The Female Guardian Society" was founded by them a year later, and a newspaper was established to present its claims. The officers were women. They visited the Tombs, and held weekly prayer-meetings. They secured the legislation necessary to bring about the separation of men and women in the city prisons, and the appointment of matrons for the women. In 1853 they procured an enactment "whereby dissipated and vicious parents, by habitually neglecting due care and provision for their offspring, shall forfeit their natural claim to them, and whereby such children shall be removed from them and placed under better influences till the claim of the parents shall be re-established by continued sobriety, industry, and general good conduct." They secured the passage of the Truant Act, and the appointment of Truant Officers. Mr. Lewis Tappan was not only the auditor for the organization, but gave effective help by suggestions that led to the establishment of the first Home for the Friendless, of which there are now seven in charge of the society. In 1854, Industrial schools were added. Cooking, housekeeping, kindergarten, and fresh-air work de-

veloped rapidly. There are now twelve industrial schools, where six thousand children are
taught. The report of the first semi-annual meeting, held in Utica, N. Y., is in quaint contrast to
the reports of the first Suffrage meetings. They
say : "The utmost harmony and union of feeling
have characterized all the proceedings, and as we
looked around and saw the intelligence and piety
and moral worth that was assembled there, and
listened to the discussion of subjects of practical
importance, while every one was manifestly seeking to know and do her duty, we could not
but feel that the most determined opposer of
'women's meetings' would have found nothing
to censure had he been present. There has been
no frivolity, no fanaticism, no disorder. We are
sure that not a wife or mother was there who was
not at least as well disposed and prepared to discharge her relative duties as she would have been
if she had kept at home."

Upon the great cause of Temperance, also, the
Woman-Suffrage movement early laid a blighting
hand. As will be remembered, total abstinence
was one of the doctrines to which many of
the no-government, common-property, men and
women were pledged. Western and Central New
York has been the birthplace of some of the wild-
est and most destructive movements that our
social life has witnessed. If the year 1848, which
saw the beginnings of the Woman-Suffrage movement, was wonderful for revolutions and insurrec-

tions the world over, the years that preceded it were remarkable, especially in this country and this State, for some of the maddest vagaries that ever have been known here. There and then arose the Shaker excitement, so fantastic that only now and then was the outside world permitted to know what was being done. Then and there Fourierism found its most fruitful field, and of the dozen or more communities that were started, several united in forming, near Rochester, an Industrial Union. John Collins started a number of vague branches of what the Fourierites called the "no-God, no-government, no-marriage, no-money, no-meat, no-salt, no-pepper" system of community. Here John H. Noyes, under the guise of a new heaven on an old earth, established his foul community at Oneida. There and then the Millerite madness sent whole congregations into the cemeteries, in white gowns, to await the sounding of the trump of Gabriel. There and then arose the great spiritualistic movement that began in Wayne County with the Fox family, became famous as the Rochester Knockings, and blossomed into communities in which "Free Love" grew out of "Individual Sovereignty." Then and there, in Wayne County, Joseph Smith pretended that the Angel Maroni had shown him, the Book of Mormon. Many of these movements were in sympathy with Woman Suffrage, and workers in them early found their way into its ranks.

In the midst of the Anti-slavery excitement, secret temperance organizations were formed among the women in New York State, known as the "Daughters of Temperance." "Finding," as they said, "that there was no law nor gospel in the land," they became a law unto themselves, and visited saloons, where they broke windows, glasses, and bottles, and threw kegs and barrels of liquor into the streets. A few were arrested, but they were soon discharged. As time went on, these secret organizations began to form themselves into regular bodies, and in January, 1852, they assembled their delegates at Albany to claim admission to the State Temperance organization, with no invitation or authority but their own. Susan B. Anthony was the first speaker, and when the convention decided not to hear her, it was announced that they would withdraw and hold a meeting where "men and women would be equal," which they accordingly did. The movement continued, until, three months later, Miss Anthony called "The New York State Temperance Convention," of which Mrs. Stanton was elected President. Among the resolutions that she introduced in her opening speech, were these: that "no woman remain in the relation of wife to a confirmed drunkard;" that the State should be petitioned so to "modify its laws affecting marriage and the custody of children, that the drunkard shall have no claims on either wife or child;" that "no liquor should be used for

culinary purposes;" and that "as charity begins
at home, let us withdraw from all associations for
sending the gospel to the heathen across the
ocean, for the education of young men for the
ministry, for the building up of a theological aristocracy and gorgeous temples to the unknown
God, and devote ourselves to the poor and suffering about us. Let us feed and clothe the naked
and hungry, gather children into schools, and
provide reading-rooms and decent homes for
young men and women thrown alone upon the
world." The organization of "The Woman's New
York State Temperance Society" was formed,
and Mrs. Stanton was elected its President. She
issued an appeal to the women of the State, and
sent a letter to the Convention at Albany which
"was so radical, that its friends feared to read
it," but Susan B. Anthony finally did so. They
elected as delegates to the "Men's New York
State Temperance Convention," to be held in
Syracuse in June, Susan B. Anthony, Mrs. Amelia
Bloomer, and Gerrit Smith. When they arrived
they were met by the Rev. Samuel J. May, who
told them that the men were shocked at the idea
of admitting them, and said that he was com-
missioned to beg them to withdraw. They
decided to present their credentials, and of course
the stormy scene which they had invited followed
their action. This scene was repeated in every
part of the State, the agitators figuring upon
their own platforms as martyrs to the noble

causes of Anti-slavery, Temperance, and Woman's
Rights. A single quotation from a letter of Miss
Anthony's, written at this time to the league,
shows that then, as now, the radical woman workers for Prohibition were nothing if not political.
She says: " And it is for woman now, in the present presidential campaign, to say to her father,
husband, or brother, ' If you vote for any candidate for any office whatever, who is not pledged
to total abstinence and the Maine law, we shall
hold you alike guilty with the rum-seller.' "

In January, 1853, a great mass-meeting was
held in Albany of all the State temperance
organizations. The Woman's society met in a
Baptist church, which was crowded at every session. Miss Anthony presided. Twenty-eight
thousand women had signed petitions for prohib-
itory legislation. The rules of the House were
suspended, and the women were invited to present
them at the speaker's desk. They were then
invited to New York, and, in Metropolitan Hall,
addressed a large audience, as well as in the
Broadway Tabernacle and Knickerbocker Hall,
Brooklyn. In the next two months they made
successful tours of many cities of the State. But,
like Mr. Garrison, and Stephen Foster, and H. C.
Wright, the women thought that if they were not
attacking and being attacked there could be no
" progress " or " reform." They demanded divorce for drunkenness, they denounced wine at
private tables, and called on the women to leave

all church organizations where "clergymen and bishops, liquor-dealers, and wine-bibbers, were dignified and honored as deacons and elders." They denounced the church for its "apathy," and the clergy for their " hostility to the public action of women," and they soon began to turn the kindly feeling that was endeavoring to work with them into enmity, and were of course denounced in their turn.

The Society decided to invite men into their organization, but not to allow them to hold office or to vote. This they did for a year, after which men were admitted to full membership. The first annual meeting of the Woman's State Temperance Society was held in Rochester, June 1, 1853, Mrs. Stanton presiding, and the attendance was larger than they had had at any time. In the course of the meetings a heated debate on the subject of divorce took place. Mrs. Stanton and Lucy Stone took the ground that it was "not only woman's right, but her duty, to withdraw from all such unholy relations," and Mrs. Nichols and Antoinette Brown opposed them.

The men were admitted to this convention, and, to use the words of the women, " it was the policy of these worldly-wise men to restrict the debate on Temperance to such narrow limits as to disturb none of the existing conditions of society." This farce in reform soon came to an end, and the following is the epitaph pronounced over it by its founders: " The society, with its guns silenced

on the popular foes, lingered a year or two, and
was heard of no more." On May 12, the friends
of Temperance met in Dr. Spring's Old Brick
Church, New York City. A motion was made
that all gentlemen present be admitted as delegates. Dr. Trall, of New York, moved an amendment, that the words "and ladies" be added, as
there were delegates present from the "Woman's
State Temperance Society." The motion was
carried, and the credentials were received. A
motion was then made that Susan B. Anthony be
added to the business committee, and all was in
an uproar at once. "Mayor Barstow twice asked
that another chairman be appointed, as he would
not preside over a meeting where woman's rights
was introduced, or women were allowed to speak."
Some of the gentlemen present said that "the
ladies were there expressly to disturb." The
ministers present, like the laymen, were divided
in opinion in regard to the admission of the delegates; but the credentials were withdrawn, and
in due time the bearers of them withdrew also.
The writers of the "History" say: "Most of the
liberal men and women now withdrew from all
temperance organizations, leaving the movement
in the hands of time-serving priests and politicians,
who, being in the majority, effectually blocked
the progress of the reform for the time—destroying, as they did, the enthusiasm of the
women in trying to press it as a political measure." Comparing this work with their Anti-

slavery campaign, they say: "When Garrison's forces had been thoroughly sifted, and only the picked men and women remained, he soon made political parties and church organizations feel the power of his burning words." It was the men and women from whom he and his were sifted who spoke the burning words that ended in burning deeds for the extinction of slavery; and thus it was with Temperance. There remained after the "sifting" many societies, of one of which William E. Dodge and President Mark Hopkins were chief officers, and John B. Gough was principal orator.

The writers of the "History" further say, in regard to the death of their organization: "Henceforward women took no active part in temperance until the Ohio Crusade revived them all over the nation, and gathered the scattered forces into the Woman's National Christian Temperance Union, of which Frances E. Willard is President." This is a mistake, for women were very active in connection with Temperance societies of which men were officers, and in organizations of their own, before and after the W. C. T. U. was founded. The history of that great body furnishes another proof of the injurious effect of the Suffrage movement upon the cause of Temperance. In 1872 a political Temperance party was formed in Columbus, Ohio, which, four years later, at Cleveland, became the Prohibition Party. From the first, this party inserted a plank in its platform favoring universal suffrage, and mentioning especially the extension of suffrage to women. The W. C. T. U. was founded as a non-denominational and non-partisan body, and was divided and sub-divided into committees, each having charge of a distinct branch of philan-thropic work, which was by no means confined solely to Temperance measures. This has given the body great working strength, and its efforts are well known. Everything except its Suffrage labor has had rich reward. I was present at the Metropolitan Opera House in New York City (in 1886, I think), and witnessed with amazement the high-handed fashion in which an organization whose constitution forbade political coalition was handed over to the Prohibition Party, pledged to give aid and comfort. The division and bitter feeling that resulted were a serious injury to the cause of Temperance. In her contribution to the volume entitled "Woman's Work in America," Miss Willard says:   " After ten years' experience, the women of this Crusade became convinced that until the people of this country divide at the ballot-box, on the foregoing [Temperance] issue, America can never be nationally delivered from the dram-shop. They therefore publicly an-nounced their devotion to the Prohibition Party, and promised to lend it their influence, which, with the exception of a very small minority, they have since most sedulously done." Writing in "The Outlook" for June 27, 1896, Lady Henry

Somerset says, in closing a sketch of Frances Willard: "The Temperance cause, in spite of the gigantic strides it has made of late years toward success, is still relegated to the shadowy land of unpopular and supposedly impracticable and visionary reform."

The Temperance cause is not relegated to a shadowy land, but has just taken, in many places, notably in New York State, another gigantic stride toward success. Prohibition has proved less faithful to the women than Miss Willard said the women had proved to it; for, in the struggle to survive the attack upon its life made by Populism in 1896, it refused to re-insert the Woman-Suffrage plank in its platform. Mrs. Helen Gougar bolted with the Populists. Mrs. Boole, of New York, in behalf of the W. C. T. U., moved the re-insertion in the platform of the Woman-Suffrage plank, which had been stricken out when it was decided to make prohibition the only issue. Amidst great confusion, Mrs. Boole was obliged to withdraw her motion, and when she changed her claim from that for a plank in the platform to one for a resolution which declared the convention to be in favor of Woman Suffrage, it was accepted by the Committee on Resolutions, and adopted with only a few dissenting votes. In view of the fact that the party has had a Suffrage plank since 1872, when it began to be, this does seem like a turning of the back rather than of the cold shoulder. When to its motto "No secta-

rianism in religion, no sectionalism in politics,"
the W. C. T. U. added "No sex in citizenship," it
fastened itself to a principle that has not progressed.    Its Temperance work "for God and
home and native land" has gone on; but the
political alliance and effort have alike proved
futile.    A striking proof of this fact is seen in the
reports of the non-political sections of the W. C.
T. U. itself.    Police matrons have been placed
through their petitions, and educational and philanthropic work that is directly in the line of doing
away with the liquor evil, and is worthy of high
praise, has been accomplished.    Miss Willard,
in her article already alluded to, reports that
"under the leadership of Mrs. Mary H. Hunt, the
W. C. T. U. has secured laws requiring scientific
temperance instruction in thirty States."    The
number is now forty-two, and I cannot help believing that Mrs. Hunt must feel more hopeful of
the favorable results to temperance of well-
directed effort to influence those who have the
power to execute the laws they pass, than Miss
Willard has reason to feel for its success through
prohibition and the forceless votes of women
whose power in philanthropy is fully recognized
and cheerfully acknowledged.    Women talk as if
the solid vote of their sex would be cast in favor
of temperance.    The census of 1890 reveals the
fact that there were in that year three times as
many woman hotel-keepers as in 1870, and seven
times as many saloon-keepers and bar-tenders.

Again, in the Nation's greatest crisis, Woman Suffrage showed itself to be the antipodes of woman's progress. Those of us whose once sable locks are now silvered are content to wear the badge of years, when we remember that we were permitted to live long enough ago to have felt the expansion of soul, the fervor of loyal love, the melting power of an overwhelming universal sorrow and a united joy, which filled the mighty days during a war for freedom and for the life of the Republic. Most of the women of the land were working with a devotion that spared neither strength nor life. What was the Woman-Suffrage Association doing? I answer in their own words. In their " History," they say: "While the most of women never philosophize on the principles that underlie national existence, there were those in our late war who understood the political significance of the struggle: the ' irrepressible conflict between freedom and slavery ; between national and State rights.' They saw that to provide lint, bandages, and supplies for the army, while the war was not conducted on a wise policy, was labor in vain ; and while many organizations, active, vigilant, self-sacrificing, were multiplied to look after the material wants of the army, these few formed themselves into a National Loyal League to teach sound principles of government, and to impress on the nation's conscience, that 'freedom to the slaves was the only way to victory.'" They further say: "Accustomed as most women had

10

been to works of charity, to the relief of outward
suffering, it was difficult to rouse their enthusiasm
for an idea, to persuade them to labor for a
principle. They clamored for practical work,
something for their hands to do ; for fairs, sewing
societies to raise money for soldiers' families, for
tableaux, readings, theatricals, anything but conventions to discuss principles and to circulate
petitions for emancipation. They could not see
that the best service they could render the army
was to suppress the rebellion, and that the most
effective way to accomplish that was to transform
the slaves into soldiers. The Woman's Loyal
League voiced the solemn lessons of the war ;
universal suffrage, and universal amnesty."

The Woman's Loyal League "voiced" the fact
that the professional agitators of the Suffrage
movement were not patriots. Again they filled
the land with words, while all the others of their
sex were blazoning the page of their country's
history with deeds of the noblest self-sacrifice, the
most gentle daring. When we remember with
what infinite patience the great emancipator was
waiting for the hour when in his wisdom he dis-
cerned that he could "best save the Union by
emancipating all the slaves," we realize what
added sorrow may have been pressed upon his
heart by the foolish petitions that the League
were rolling up by the hundred thousand and
sending to a Congress that was powerless to heed
them if it would. Statesmen and Generals were

staggered by the stupendous task of guiding a great people and saving the Union in the most powerful rebellion ever known; but these few women knew from the beginning that "the war was not conducted on a wise policy," and that to provide for the army was "labor in vain." They joined the great body of fault-finders and talkers, and lifted not a finger in practical work. And they are the women who would fain vote for and become America's rulers! The "other women," who were narrow-minded enough to prepare stores and raise money for the army, and do such concrete work as nursing in the hospital and on the field, had been busy for nearly two years when the Suffrage women bestirred themselves in their own way. In March, 1863, they issued the following appeal to the "Loyal Women of the Nation," which I quote at length because it is an excellent example of their methods, which "began in words and ended in words :"

"In this crisis of our country's destiny, it is the duty of every citizen to consider the peculiar blessings of a republican form of government, and decide what sacrifices of wealth and life are demanded for its defence and preservation. The policy of the war, our whole future life, depends on a clearly-defined idea of the end proposed, and the immense advantages to be secured to ourselves and all mankind by its accomplishment. No mere party or sectional cry, no technicalities of constitution or military law, no mottoes of craft

or policy, are big enough to touch the great heart
of a nation in the midst of revolution. A grand
idea, such as freedom or justice, is needful to
kindle and sustain the fires of a high enthusiasm.
At this hour the best word and work of every
man and woman are imperatively demanded. To
man, by common consent, is assigned the forum,
camp, and field. What is woman's legitimate
work, and how she may best accomplish it, is
worthy of our earnest counsel with one another.
We have heard many complaints of the lack of
enthusiasm among Northern women; but, when
a mother lays her son on the altar of her country,
she asks an object equal to the sacrifice. In nursing the sick and wounded, knitting socks, scrap-
ing lint and making jellies, the bravest and best
may weary if the thoughts mount not in faith to
something beyond and above it all. ‚Work is ·
worship only when a noble purpose fills the soul.‵›
Woman is equally interested and responsible with
man in the final settlement of this problem of self-
government; therefore let none stand idle specta-
tors now. When every hour is big with destiny,
and each delay but complicates our difficulties, it
is high time for the daughters of the Revolution,
in solemn council, to unseal the last will and testament of the Fathers—lay hold of their birth-
right of freedom, and keep it a sacred trust for
all coming generations. To this end we ask the
Loyal Women of the Nation to meet in the church
of the Puritans (Dr. Cheever's), New York, on

Thursday, the 14th of May next." This was signed by Elizabeth Cady Stanton, and Susan B. Anthony, in behalf of the Woman's Central Committee.

Having set forth their belief that by common consent the forum, the camp, and the field were assigned to men, these women secured a forum from which to promulgate advice and direction to the men who were indeed allowed possession of the camp and the field. After a speech, in which, among other things, Miss Anthony said: "Instead of suppressing the real cause of the war, it should have been proclaimed, not only by the people, but by the President, Congress, Cabinet, and every military commander," she presented resolutions, which included this:

"Resolved: that there can never be a true peace in this Republic until all the civil and political rights of all citizens of African descent and all women are practically established."

The reading of the resolutions was followed by one of the long, acrimonious debates with which those who read the reports of their conventions are familiar. They resented it bitterly when Mrs. Hoyt, of Wisconsin, said: "The women of the North were invited here to meet in convention, not to hold a Temperance meeting, not to hold an Anti-slavery meeting, not to hold a Woman's Rights convention, but to consult as to the best practical way for the advancement of the loyal cause. We have a great many very flourishing

Loyal Leagues throughout the West, and we have
kept them sacred from Anti-slavery, Woman's
Rights, Temperance, and everything else, good
though they may be. In our League we have
several objects in view. The first is, retrench-
ment in household expenses, to the end that the
material resources of the Government may be, so
far as possible, applied to the entire and thorough vindication of its authority. Second, to
strengthen the loyal sentiment of the people at
home, and instil a deeper love of the National flag.
The third and most important object is to write
to the soldiers in the field, thus reaching nearly
every private in the army, to encourage and
stimulate him in the way that ladies know how
to do." After expressions of strong resentment,
those who had called the convention returned to
their generalizing in regard to the duty and influence of woman, and to denunciations of the
Government for its conduct of the war. The resolutions which had called forth the strictures
were accepted, and Miss Anthony announced that
" The resolution recommending practical work
was not yet prepared." It was written at a business meeting following, and read thus:

" Resolved, that we, loyal women of the nation,
do hereby pledge ourselves one to another, in a
Loyal League, to give support to the Government
in so far as it makes the war a war for freedom."

If the Government of the United States had received no more practical pledges, from no more

loyal hearts than these, there would have been little reward for the patriotic devotion that laid down life in defence of the Union. A sentiment that was often expressed by the Suffragist was that as woman had no vote she could not properly be called upon to be loyal. The "practical" work finally accomplished was the gathering of another monster petition, in which they told President Lincoln that " Northern power and loyalty can never be measured until the purpose of the war be liberty to man." To the close of the war they did nothing but sign such petitions.

I turn to Dr. Brockett's great book, " Woman in the Civil War," and I find recorded the names and the work of four hundred and eighty-four women who gave invaluable and honorable special service, some of them even to the sacrifice of life itself ; and of all this number, only a half dozen are known in Suffrage annals.

Cure by ballot has been the one and only remedy suggested by Suffrage conventions for all the ills, real or imaginary, that are endured by women. As long ago as 1854, in a convention in Philadelphia, they uttered the same sentiment. In commenting upon Mrs. Jane G. Swisshelm's book, "Half a Century," they say : " While ever and anon during the last forty years Mrs. Swisshelm has seized some of these dilettante literary women with her metaphysical tweezers, and held them up to scorn for their ridicule of the Woman Suffrage conventions, yet in her own recently

published work, in her mature years, she vouch-
safes no words of approval for those who have
inaugurated the greatest movement of the centuries. . . . It is quite evident from her last pro-
nunciamento that she has no just appreciation of
the importance and dignity of our demand for
justice and equality. A soldier without a leg is a
fact so much more readily understood than all
women without ballots, and his loss so much more
readily comprehended and supplied, that we can
hardly blame any one for doing the work of the
hour, rather than struggling a lifetime for an
idea. Hence it is not a matter of surprise that
most women are more readily enlisted in the sup-
pression of evils in the concrete, than in advocat-
ing the principles that underlie them in the
abstract, and thus ultimately choosing the broader
and more lasting work."

In her "Reminiscences," contributed to the
"History," Mrs. Emily Collins says: "From 1858
to 1869 my home was in Rochester, N. Y. There,
by brief newspaper articles and in other ways, I
sought to influence public sentiment in favor of
this fundamental reform. In 1868 a society was
organized there for the reformation of abandoned
women. At one of its meetings I endeavored to
show how futile all their efforts would be while
women, by the laws of the land, were made a
subject class."

This was typical action. Thus it was in Anti-
slavery, thus in Temperance, thus in the Civil

War, and thus it has been with general reforms.
What Suffragists have deemed to be an abstract
"right" has prevented them from taking active
part in any efforts put forth to end a concrete
wrong. As time goes on, this spirit becomes
more injurious, because progress is carrying philanthropy into higher fields of moral action, and
in so doing is carrying it away from and above
the plane where rests the ballot-box. While Suffrage effort is directed toward keeping all issues
in the political arena, the trend of legislation is
to take them out of politics. By the public votes
of men and the private votes and public appeals
of women, philanthropic and educational matters
are being removed from the uncertainties and
fluctuations of party action. As they are thus
brought out of the sphere where woman is powerless and into that in which it is natural for her
to act, the whole force of sympathy, and her
ability to picture and to pursue an ideal, are
finding exercise and are hastening the day
when there will be no slavery, no drunkenness, no
war, and no violation of woman's chastity. Dr.
Jacobi, in her volume, says: "Why should we
wonder at the low tone which habitually prevails in relation to public affairs, when the
women who stand as guardians at the fountain
sources and household shrines of thought are
trained to believe that there are no Rights, but
only Privileges, Expediencies, Immunities? Can
those who cower before the public ridicule which

greets the enunciation of the Rights of Women; who are habituated to stifle generous impulses for their own larger freedom at the authoritative dictation of the men they see in power,—can such women be relied upon to nerve the Nation's heart for generous deeds?" Who were trained by women at the fountain sources and household shrines? The very men whom they now see in "authoritative dictation." And so well did they train them that when both are called upon to nerve the nation's heart for generous deeds, they act together—the trainer and the trained—moved by the same magnetic impulse of a noble devotion. It is purely gratuitous to assume, because women generally have discredited the dogma of Woman Suffrage, that they have therefore no just conception of rights. Women are as ambitious, as self-assertive, as are men. They deal more naturally with abstractions, and are more tenacious of purpose. They are impatient of hindrance, and it is inconsistent with facts to infer that they have been "stifling generous impulses for their own larger freedom," at the dictation of their own sons. The executive power and wisdom of these sons they feel to be the very thing they most desire for them, a reward for their own abounding faith and love. Privileges, Expediencies, and Immunities are their Rights. How well fitted such rights are to enable them to nerve the Nation's heart was seen in the great crisis we have been considering, when the ignoble dogma of Suffrage caused its believers to fail in generous impulse and to stand aloof in the time of a supreme need.

I cannot agree with Dr. Jacobi that a low tone habitually prevails in relation to public affairs. The guards freshly thrown about the ballot, and the greater watchfulness over entrance to citizenship, are two of the most obvious advances at this moment.

# CHAPTER V.

In the fourth and fifth counts of the Declaration of Sentiments, the Suffragists say : " Having deprived her of this first right of a citizen, the elective franchise, thereby leaving her without representation in the halls of legislation, he has oppressed her on all sides." " He has made her, if married, in the eye of the law, civilly dead."

The following four counts all refer to a married woman's civil deadness; and I will give them in order, and then consider the five counts together :

" He has taken from her all right in property, even to the wages she earns." " He has made her, morally, an irresponsible being, as she can commit many crimes with impunity, provided they be done in the presence of her husband." " In the covenant of marriage, she is compelled to promise obedience to her husband, he becoming, to all intents and purposes, her master—the law giving him power to deprive her of her liberty, and to administer chastisement." " He has. so framed the laws of divorce, as to what shall be proper

156

causes, and, in case of separation, to whom the guardianship of the children shall be given, as to be wholly regardless of the happiness of women —the law, in all cases, going upon a false supposition of the supremacy of man, and giving all power into his hands."

That the women did not find themselves, as might be supposed from their charges, living under the edicts of the Middle Ages, is proved by their hunt through statute-books for such of the eighteen grievances as relate to laws.  They also say that " while they had felt the insults incident to sex, in many ways, as every proud thinking woman must, yet they had not in their own experience endured the coarser forms of tyranny resulting from unjust laws; but had souls large enough to feel the wrongs of others."  Until they knew what those wrongs were, it would seem they could hardly have felt for them intelligently. It would seem, too, that the great body of American women were also unaware that they had been, and were still being, legally and morally robbed, enslaved, and murdered.  In fact, Suffrage speakers have been compelled to account for their unconcern by considering it the result of long subjection, and at the same time have had to claim that these stupid beings were fit to rule with and over men.

While the counts contain concrete statements, the closing clause—" the law in all cases, going upon a false supposition of the supremacy of man,

and giving all power into his hands"—sets forth
an abstract idea in justification of which they
furnish no proof.  In the counts as they stood in
the Declaration of Sentiments, the general laws
were not accused of doing any injustice, personal
or civil, to an unmarried woman, except in reference to the one matter of withholding the vote,
which they claimed was wrong because she had
an inalienable right to the ballot and was subject
to tax.  Not a personal law did they ask to have
changed for her protection.  They recognized the
fact that, unless she was married, a woman in the
United States stood upon a legal equality with
man.  The hue and cry in regard to a married
woman was, that she was not treated as if *femme
sole*.  The *femme sole* could make contracts and
wills, sue and be sued, and do all and sundry in
her own name that her brother could do.  With
a married woman the situation was different.
Will any one contend that in the past the married
woman has been held in less honor than the unmarried?  Can it be thought for a moment that
the law-makers expressed their contempt for
wives and mothers, and their respect for daughters
and sisters who were unmarried?  Tradition and
fact, poetry and prose, romance and reality, all
go to prove that the reverential feeling of the
world has gathered about the wife and the
mother.  The men who made those laws turned
for their ideals of abstract justice to their mothers'
faith and teaching; and it seems most incongruous

to assume, as do the Suffrage arguments, that, while all the laws relating to women were tyrannical at some point, those in regard to married women were the ones wherein men embodied their most cruel and revengeful feeling. It also appears to be a gratuitous assumption that whatever was different in the legal treatment of men and women came from man's belief in his own supremacy, especially toward the wife into whose hands he had committed the keeping of his home and his honor.

In 1881, after more than thirty years of agitation of the subject, the Suffrage leaders said: " The condition of married women under the laws of all countries has been essentially that of slaves, until modified in some respects, within the last quarter of a century, in the United States." And again they said : " The change from the old common law of England, in regard to the civil rights of women, from 1848 to the advance legislation in most of the Northern States in 1880, marks an era both in the status of woman as a citizen and in our American system of jurisprudence. When the State of New York gave married women certain rights of property, the individual existence of the wife was recognized, and the old idea that husband and wife are one, and that one the husband, received its death-blow. From that hour the statutes of the several States have been steadily diverging from the old English codes. Most of the Western States copied the advance legislation of New York, and some are now even more liberal."

This sentence contains another of the constantly recurring instances of the methods by which the Suffrage mind jumps to unwarranted conclusions. When the State of New York gave married women certain property rights, it recognized their legal existence in a new way, but not their individual existence—that had been recognized by every act of law and custom, from the registry of their birth to that of their marriage or their death. Socially and civilly, every woman in the United States had had opportunity to make her individuality felt, and if there was any difference in advantage in respect of this, it was supposed to lie with the married woman. So true is this, that Mrs. Stanton and Mrs. Mott had to hunt for oppressive laws, and most of the women of this land have no real sense of the great and liberal change in laws concerning married women since 1848. I am no more approving of or admiring the old English common law, or the canon law, concerning women, than I am approving of or admiring the law that came to light recently in the Transvaal and would have allowed the torture of Jameson and his men, who, as a matter of fact, were allowed to go almost unpunished. The law of the Dutch Government in Africa belonged to the Middle Ages; their conduct belonged to to-day. I only believe that at the time when it was possible for one man to frame for another man such laws of physical and mental torment as every code reveals, their laws for women were the best they could devise, and were those which led to the freedom of the women of to-day. A law of England still favors only the first-born son, and he only because he is the first-born. What wonder that girls have been denied succession; and what an evidence of man's desire to show favor and not the "insult incident to sex," that he has placed woman on thrones upon which he has had to sustain her by main force.

There is no need that I should darken my pages with the English laws concerning married women. The Suffrage leaders have spread them abroad; Blackstone says they were intended for woman's protection and benefit, and adds the remark, "So great a favorite is the female sex with the laws of England." If I quoted them, I should be constrained to quote barbarous laws concerning men of the same era, and to note the lack of all laws concerning the brute creation; for neither of these matters is touched by Suffrage writers. Dr. Jacobi is willing to say that "in the eye of the law, the married white woman in the North was as devoid of personality as the African slave . in the South," and she also says: "By another error of interpretation, certain laws which remain on the statute-book, or which have been recently added, have been considered so peculiarly favorable to women, that they are thought to prove a legislative tendency to grant special immunities to

11

women so long as they consent to remain unfranchised." Does she mean to say that the law-makers have asked the women if they would consent to remain unfranchised? I thought that leaving them unfranchised without asking their consent was, in Suffrage eyes, the very front of the offending. The laws that remain on the statute-book, and those that have been recently added, go to prove to my mind that the old laws were meant to be generous as well as just; second, that the trend of legislation *is* peculiarly favorable to woman; and, thirdly, that those laws which between man and man might be looked upon as offsets to suffrage equality, between man and woman could not be so considered. They were, therefore, proper immunities for persons whose consent was not asked through the vote because, in the nature of the difference between the sexes, a prime requisite for compliance was lacking. Dr. Jacobi goes on to say: "The fear has been expressed that these 'immunities' and 'privileges' would be forfeited were the franchise conferred. And this fear has actually been advanced as an argument—as the basis of protest against equal suffrage." Either the law is tyrannical to women, or it is not. If Suffrage leaders are actually talking of its privileges and immunities to women, and trying to explain them away, we may leave the burden of proof to them. But as to the gist of her remark in regard to the connection between legal privileges and equal suffrage : Fear of losing the legal immunities that are granted to both married and unmarried women on account of their attitude as wards of the State when they are not able to assume the first duty implied in giving up the wardship—that of physical defence to themselves and others—is a most legitimate fear, and is a sound reason for protest against equal suffrage. Wrapped up with the legal privileges of women are those of their children—the rights of minors. For boys, special privileges cease at the age of twenty-one. For girls, they do not. Legal equality would set the boy and the girl on the same level at once. The law of equality could know no such thing as " exemption " for the unmarried woman, or " dower right " or " maintenance " for the married woman that would not be equally binding on both husband and wife. In Germany, rich American women are maintaining their land-poor husbands under legal stress, " in the style to which they have been accustomed," because the law of Germany is " equal " in respect to property maintenance of husband and wife. In Ohio, where Suffrage agitation has been persistent, the legislature in 1894 passed an act " enabling a husband, as well as a wife, to sue and obtain alimony pending divorce proceedings."

We began by talking of legal disabilities, and, led by the Suffragists themselves, are already discussing legal immunities.

The editors of the " History " say : " The laws

affecting woman's civil rights have been greatly improved during the past thirty years, but the political demand has made but questionable progress, though it must be counted as the chief influence in modifying the laws. The selfishness of man was readily enlisted in securing woman's civil rights, while the same element in his character antagonized her demand for political equality." If it was his selfishness that procured woman civil rights and privileges, was it his unselfishness that formerly denied them? The fact that the States that granted them first, and most fully, are the ones where Suffrage has made least progress, suggests the injustice of the charge.

But a question of real interest is, must the political demand made by women be counted as the chief influence in modifying the laws?

In 1836, Judge Hertell presented, in the New York Legislature, a bill to secure property rights to married women, which had been drawn up under the supervision of the Hon. John Savage, Chief Justice of the Supreme Court, and the Hon. John C. Spencer, one of the revisers of the statutes. In its behalf Ernestine Rose and Paulina Wright Davis circulated a petition, to which they gained only five signatures among their own sex.

Ernestine Rose was a Polish Jewess who had renounced all faith with her own. She was an extreme communist, and before coming here to labor for Liberalism and Woman Suffrage, she had presided over a body called " An Association of all Classes of all Nations, without distinction of sect, sex, party condition, or color." Paulina Wright Davis, gifted though she was, was a radical of an extreme type. How much the character of the advocates had to do with their failure, it is impossible to say, but it appears to be another proof of the evil influence of Suffrage action upon woman's progress that so good a work should have been in hands so unfitted for it. The bill did not become a law. Mrs. Rose records that she continued to send petitions with increased numbers of signatures until 1848–49; that from 1837 to 1848 she addressed the New York Legislature five times, and a good many times after the latter date. That she was not recognized as an aid to legislation seems evident from the testimony that follows.

In the previous chapter I have quoted the editors of the " History " as saying that the first thing that led them to demand political rights was the discussion, in several of the State legislatures, of these property questions in regard to married women. Another proof that they did not inspire the early laws is seen in the following extracts from a letter from the Hon. George Geddes, written to Mrs. Gage, in 1880, and answering her question as to who was responsible for the Married-Woman's Property-Rights bill, which was passed in 1848. He said :

" I have very distinct recollections of the whole

history of this very radical measure.  Judge Fine,
of St. Lawrence, was its originator, and he gave
me his reasons for introducing the bill.  He said
that he married a lady who had some property of
her own, which he had, all his life, tried to keep
distinct from his, that she might have the benefit
of her own, in the event of any disaster happening
to him in pecuniary matters.  He had found much
difficulty, growing out of the old laws, in this
effort to protect his wife's interests. . . . I, too,
had special reasons for desiring this change in the
law.  I had a young daughter, who, in the then
condition of my health, was quite likely to be left
in tender years without a father, and I very much
desired to protect her in the little property I
might be able to leave. . . . I believe this law
originated with Judge Fine, without any outside
prompting.  On the third day of the session he
gave notice of his intention to introduce it, and
only one petition was presented in favor of the
bill, and that came from Syracuse, and was due
to the action of my personal friends. . . . We all
felt that the laws regulating married women's, as
well as married men's, rights demanded careful
revision and adaptation to our times and to our
civilization. . . . In reply to your inquiries in regard to debates that preceded the action of 1848,
I must say I know of none, and I am quite sure
that in our long discussions no allusion was made
to anything of the kind."

It would thus appear that neither Mrs. Gage,

nor Mrs. Stanton, nor Miss Anthony knew the
names of the proposer and defenders of the bill
that opened the way in New York for all the
liberal legislation that has followed, and thirty
years after its passage they inquired whether any
debates had preceded it. Certainly, then, their
own had not. It is also evident how much "selfishness" prompted the bill.

In a pamphlet published by the New York
Woman-Suffrage Association to report their proceedings during the Constitutional Convention of
1894, it is recorded that Mr. F. B. Church, of
Alleghany, presented an appeal from his county
asking for the suffrage. In the course of his remarks he said: " Sir, beginning in 1848, the male
citizens of the State of New York, not at the
clamor of the women, as I understand it, but actu-
ated by a sense of justice, began to remove the disabilities under which women labored at that time.
Gradually, from that time on, the barriers had
been stricken away, until, in 1891, I believe, the
last impediments were removed."

In 1844, Rhode Island had passed property laws
for married women. In 1848–9 Connecticut and
Texas, as well as New York, did so, apparently
uninfluenced by anything except their "sense
of justice." In 1850–'52 Alabama and Maine
passed such laws. In 1853 New Hampshire,
Indiana, Wisconsin, and Iowa changed their laws
in this respect. They moved forward in this
reform, as did the other States, before there

was even a beginning of Suffrage agitation in them.

In 1847, Mrs. C. J. H. Nichols, who afterward became a Suffrage worker, addressed to the voters of Vermont a series of editorials setting forth the property disabilities of women. In October of that year, Hon. Larkin Mead, moved, he said, by her presentation, introduced a bill into the Senate, which, becoming a law, secured to the wife real estate owned by her at marriage, or acquired by gift, devise, or inheritance during marriage, with the rents, issues, and profits, as against any debts of the husband ; but to make a sale or conveyance of either her realty or its use valid, it must be the joint act of husband and wife. She might by last will and testament dispose of her lands, tenements, hereditaments, and any interest therein descendable to her heirs, as if "sole." Mrs. Nichols says that in 1852 she drew up a petition signed by more than two hundred business men and tax-paying widows, asking the Legislature to make women voters in school matters. Mrs. Nichols's report is clear, sound, definite, and she seems to have been of real service, and to have won what she sought. She says, "Up to 1850 I had not taken position for suffrage, although I had shown the absurdity of regarding it as unwomanly." She appears to have done a great deal of clever as well as earnest and spirited talking in the West, after she had " taken position for suffrage," and she reports that, when she removed to Kansas, her claims were for "equal educational rights and privileges in all the schools and institutions of learning fostered or controlled by the State." "An equal right in all matters pertaining to the organization and conduct of the common schools." "Recognition of the mother's equal right with the father to the control and custody of their mutual offspring." "Protection in person, property, and earnings for married women and widows, the same as for men." The first three were fully granted, the fourth was changed as to "personal service." In her pleading for "political rights," she was associated with John O. Wattles, and the amendment they proposed was defeated in the Legislature.

Petitions for "Woman's Right" and changes of the laws were circulated in Massachusetts as early as 1848. In 1849, a year after the first Suffrage Convention, Ohio, Maine, Indiana, and Missouri, had passed laws giving to married women the right to their own earnings. A "Memorial" was sent by the Suffrage Association to the Ohio Constitutional Convention in 1850, from which I take the following: "We believe the whole theory of the common law in relation to woman is unjust and degrading." (Then follows political injustice.) "We would especially call your attention to the legal condition of married women." (Then follow general statements and quotations from the common law.) The attention of the memorialists was called by the proper authorities to the fact that the statute laws of Ohio had radically changed the general matters charged. In answering comment, Mrs. Coe said : " The committee were perfectly aware of the existence of the statutes mentioned, but did not see fit to incorporate them in the petition, not only on account of their great length, but because they do not at all invalidate the position which the petition affects to establish—the inequality of the sexes before the law ; because if the wife departs from the conditions of the statutes, and thus comes under the common law, they are against her." She then adds : " There are other laws which might be mentioned, which really give woman an apparent advantage over man ; yet, having no relevancy to the subject in the petition, we did not see fit to introduce them."

The ignorance displayed here is phenomenal. Common law is operative only in the absence of statute law. The Ohio statute (as with all statutes) superseded the common law ; and if the woman " departs from the condition of the statute," she suffers the penalty prescribed therein, without reference to her previous position before the law.

One of the earliest demands made by the Suffrage Association was for a law that should allow of absolute divorce for drunkenness; and this was soon followed by demands for divorce for other causes. In presenting a petition to the New York Legislature, pressing these measures, Mrs. Stanton addressed the Assembly, and from her remarks I take the following words: " Allow me to call the attention of that party now so much interested in the slave of the Carolinas to the similarity in his condition and that of the mothers, wives, and daughters of the Empire State. The negro has no name. He is Cuffy Douglas, or Cuffy Brooks, just whose Cuffy he may chance to be. The woman has no name. She is Mrs. Richard Roe, or Mrs. John Doe, just whose Mrs. she may chance to be. Cuffy has no right to his earnings; he cannot buy or sell, nor make contracts, nor lay up anything that he can call his own. Mrs. Roe has no right to her earnings ; she can neither buy, sell, nor make contracts, nor lay up anything that she can call her own. Cuffy has no right to his children; they may be bound out to cancel a father's debts of honor. The white unborn child, even by the last will of the father, may be placed under the guardianship of a stranger, a foreigner. Cuffy has no legal right to existence; he is sub-ject to restraint and moderate chastisement. Mrs. Roe has no legal existence; she has not the best right to her person. The husband has the power to restrain and administer moderate chastisement. The prejudice against color, of which we hear so much, is no stronger than that against sex. It is produced by the same cause, and manifested very much in the same way. The negro's skin and the woman's sex are both *prima facie* evidence that they were intended to be in subjection to the white Saxon man. The few social privileges which the man gives the woman, he makes up to the negro in civil rights. The woman may sit at the same table and eat with the white man ; the free negro may hold property and vote."

It is difficult for our thought to reach the low level from which this comparison is made. It ignores all the moral and spiritual conceptions that gave rise to and hallow marriage. But looking upon marriage as a mere financial compact, and taking the laws even as they then were, a few things may be said. " Cuffy has no name that he can call his own." Elizabeth Cady Stanton has her own baptismal name, the name of her honored father, and that of her honored husband, and the opportunity to make those names more her own by personal achievement than any one's else. Her mother, her father, her husband, and her son are as dependent upon her for preserving the character and distinctiveness of that name, as she is upon them. Why Lucy Stone should have put inconvenience and indignity upon both herself and her husband for the sake of continuing to wear her father's name instead of assuming her husband's, I never could understand. She did not share the name she gave her child. And there is another distinction between the nameless Cuffy and the trebly-named Saxon woman. The husband's name was not thrust upon her. By uttering the simple monosyllable " No," she could decline to wear it. It was only as she consented to be mistress of a husband's heart and home that she passed from the condition of *femme sole* and acquired a title and an additional name. "Cuffy has no right to his earnings." This would be of less consequence to Cuffy if he had a right to his master's earnings. When a right to another's earnings goes along with the mutual relation toward a home of master and mistress, the difference between Cuffy and Mrs. Roe is unspeakable. "Cuffy cannot buy or sell, make contracts, nor lay up anything that he can call his own." If Cuffy had the right to prevent his master from buying, selling, making contracts, or laying up anything that he could call his own until Cuffy's wants had been provided for in the most ample manner, the world would have felt less moved over Cuffy's wrongs. "Cuffy has no right to his children." Mrs. Roe has a right to compel Mr. Roe to bestow his name upon her children, and to support the boys until they are twenty-one, and the girls forever. "Cuffy has no legal right to existence." Mrs. Roe has so much legal right to existence that she stands toward the State and toward her husband in the relation of a preferred creditor. The State cannot call upon her for its most arduous duties, which must however be performed in her behalf. Her husband cannot dispose of real property without her signature. If he dies solvent, nothing can prevent her taking a fair share of his estate, and he may give her the whole ; but if he dies bankrupt, neither his will, nor the State, nor

anything else, can make her pay one dollar of his
debts. " Cuffy is subject to restraint and moderate chastisement." " The husband has the power
to restrain and administer moderate chastisement."
The public horsewhipping of a husband by his
wife is a rare sight, but when it occurs the law is
far more ready to overlook the breach of order
than it is to permit the slightest attempt at assault and battery upon the wife. As the remaining statements have no reference to the laws, I
may excuse myself from telling how strangely
beneath the dignity of truth they seem to me.
That they were urged in connection with a bill
asking for divorce for drunkenness suggests that
such a plea was made an entering wedge for the
radical divorce measures that have been advocated in Suffrage conventions. Any State would,
at that time, grant legal separation for a wife
from a drunken husband, and would compel the
husband to support the wife to the extent of his
means.

This matter of easier divorce has been pressed
steadily from the beginning, but with very little
of the result that the Suffragists desired.

In the Convention of the National Council of
Women, which met in Washington, D. C., in
February, 1895, the Suffrage Associations were
largely represented. Their committee on divorce
reform consisted of Ellen Battelle Dietrick, Chairman, and Mary A. Livermore and Fanny B. Ames.
Their report was, in part, as follows: " In ac-

cordance with the instructions of the Executive Committee of the Council, your chairman sent forty-eight letters to the Governors of States and Territories, asking each to call the attention of his legislature to the situation concerning divorce laws, and requesting the appointment of a committee to consider the matter, said committee to consist of an equal number of men and women."

Here it is the same old story. Theirs is not an intelligent presentment of changes desired, but simply a continued urging of women for personal share in the making of the laws. In commenting upon the refusal of the Governor of Iowa, among others, the Committee says: "And yet Iowa is one of the States which has recently formed a commission of men to consider making Iowa divorce laws uniform with those of all other States." The laws that make it possible for a woman divorced in one State to be looked upon in another State as still bound, were not petitioned against.

Uniformity in the divorce laws of the United States is one of the great legislative reforms that are moving slowly but surely; and with that, it appears, the Suffrage appeal has nothing to do. The Committee closed its report by saying: "We might as well face the fact that the official servants of the United States cherish frank contempt for woman's opinions and wishes, and that, too, in regard to a matter which concerns the welfare of women far more vitally than it does the welfare of men. The one thing we should deprecate is having men make any new laws or fresh provisions for women's protection."

In the spring of 1854 Miss Anthony and Ernestine Rose presented a petition to the New York Legislature, and the Albany " Argus," of March 4, published a résumé of their appeal. The demands were : That husband and wife should be tenants in common of property, without survivorship, but with a partition on the death of one; that a wife should be competent to discharge trusts and powers the same as a single woman; that the statute in respect to a married woman's property be changed so that her property could descend as though she had been unmarried ; that married women should be entitled to execute letters testamentary, and of administration ; that married women should have power to make contracts and transact business as though unmarried; that they should be entitled to their own earnings, subject to their proportional liability for support of children; that post-nuptial acquisitions should belong equally to husband and wife ; that married women should stand on the same footing as single women, as parties or witnesses in legal proceedings; that they should be sole guardians of the minor children ; that the homestead should be inviolable and inalienable for widows and children ; that the laws in relation to divorce should be revised, and drunkenness made cause for absolute divorce ; that better care should be taken of single

women's property, that their rights might not be
lost through ignorance ; that the preference of
males in the descent of real estate should be
abolished ; that women should exercise the right
of suffrage, and be eligible to all offices, occupations, and professions, and to act as jurors ; that
courts of conciliation should be organized as peace-
makers ; that a law should be enacted extending
the masculine designation in all statutes of the
State to females.

I cannot fully understand Miss Anthony's position ; but in some notable particulars, not her laws
but better ones are in force. When Miss Anthony
wrote to inquire who was responsible for repealing an act of 1860 for which she had worked with
her well-known zeal, Judge Charles J. Folger replied, in part : "I think—with deference I say it
—that you are not strictly accurate in calling
the legislation of 1862 a repealing one. In but
one thing did it repeal, in the sense of taking away
right or power or privilege or freedom that the
Act of 1860 gave. On the contrary, in some respects it gave more or greater."

Miss Anthony says, in comment on Judge
Folger's letter : " Mr. Folger makes mistakes in
regard to the effect of these bills ; quite forgetting
that the wife has never had an equal right to the
joint earnings of the copartnership, as no valua-
tion has ever been placed on her labor in the
household, to which she gives all her time,
thought, and strength. A law securing to the

12

wife the absolute right to half the joint earnings, and, at the death of the husband, the same control of property and children that he has when she dies, might make some show of justice; but it is a provision not yet on the statute-books of any civilized nation."

If it were to be placed on the statute-book, would not one have to be placed beside it making the wife equally responsible for the support of the husband? The law can only take cognizance of the earnings of that member of the firm who transacts business with the outside world. How the proceeds of mutual labor shall be best made their own is for each husband and wife to settle; it cannot be matter of legislation. It is interesting to think what an increase of domesticity there would be if a business partnership, such as Miss Anthony suggests, were demanded by the statutes. The law, which now lays the whole support on the husband and father, whether the wife and daughter work in the home or not, would make it obligatory for the home partner to give all her time, thought, and strength to labor in the household, in order to bring in her bill for services.

The real test of the working of woman suffrage is to be found in the answer to the question whether better laws have been framed as a consequence?

There has been no advance in legislation in Utah or Wyoming through the action or votes of women. The authorities whom I have consulted do not know of any legislation in Colorado which can be traced directly to the presence of women in the legislature. Exception may possibly be made in regard to the Age-of-Consent bill, which, in common with nearly all the States, Colorado passed in favor of raising the age. That bill was introduced by a woman member, and was strongly advocated by the others, and it called forth an unwise discussion and a repulsive scene in the House. A great many women have been elected to county offices, in that State, especially those connected with the schools, and those of Clerk and Treasurer. In answer to a question, my correspondent adds: "I do not know of any great improvements of any kind or description in our county affairs that have been made in the past four years."

In Wyoming, where women have voted so many years, less restraint is imposed on liquor-selling than in most of the other States. Divorce is granted for any one of eleven causes, after a residence of but six months. The age of consent was only fourteen years as late as 1890. Gambling is legal; not only do the laws mention many games with cards as lawful, but a statute declares: "No town, city, or municipal corporation in this Territory shall hereafter have power to prohibit, suppress or regulate any gaming-house or game, licensed as provided for in this chapter." "Excusable homicide" is also defined by statute. It is allowable "when committed by accident or misfortune, in the heat of passion or sufficient provocation, or upon a sudden combat; provided that no undue advantage is taken, nor any dangerous weapon used, and that the killing is not done in a cruel or unusual manner." The laws could hardly have been worse before women voted.

It is matter of surprise to find how generally in Western towns and States in which woman has voted or held office, "Woman has degraded politics, and politics has degraded woman." This is not, to my mind, proof that American women are degenerating, but it suggests that the women who have sought political life are not representative.

Another legal demand very early made by the Suffrage leaders was that for the entrance of women into men's colleges. So far as the State could control this by law, it has done so. Every educational institution that receives State support, from the primary school to the State University, is now open to women. Cornell University, opened in October, 1868, was aided by a State gift of a million acres, and opened its doors to women in April, 1872. In the West, the State Universities would have been closed for lack of pupils, during the war, if women had not attended them.

The New York State Suffrage Association includes in its report of the doings at the Constitutional Convention a report of its legislative work for the twenty-two years of its existence. Of the many petitions presented during those years, but three relate to anything but Suffrage in some form, and these did not originate with the New York Suffrage Association. One of these three related to the bill to secure police matrons in New York City. Work was begun in 1882 and ended in success in 1891, there being strong opposition to it. The act to provide woman physicians for prisons, and one making mother and father joint guardians of children, passed in 1888 and 1892. Three of the Suffrage bills refer to school matters, one of which was successful and two were lost. Five relate to municipal suffrage, all of which were defeated. The remaining sixteen bills were all for full suffrage, were all urged by many speakers, and were all defeated. I give, in closing, Mr. Francis M. Scott's summary of the laws of New York State that relate especially to women and are in force to-day. Much special legislation urged by Suffrage petitions has not been enacted at all, and much has been passed in a different form. Suffragists say that the change of laws constitutes no reason for opposing suffrage, but to my mind it constitutes a most excellent one. What has been done by petition proves the power to do more by the same means, and the fact that much of the best legislation has been against the demand of the Suffragists or in precedence of it, proves that the rights of women are in hands that are capable of meeting fresh interests as they arise.

Every profession and business is open to women

to exactly the same extent as to men, and already women have found a place in law, medicine, architecture, journalism, and other professions.

Single women always could engage in commercial and mercantile pursuits without hindrance or restriction.

Notwithstanding her marriage, a woman now holds and enjoys her separate property, however acquired, freed from any interference or control on the part of her husband, and from all liability for his debts.

She may sell, assign, and transfer her real and personal property, and carry on any trade or business and perform any labor and services on her own sole and separate account, and her earnings are her own sole and separate property.

She may sue and be sued, as if she were unmarried, and may maintain an action in her own name for injury to her person or character (including actions for slander or libel), and the proceeds of any such action are her sole and separate property.

She may contract to the same extent, with like effect in the same form as if she were unmarried, and she and her separate estate are liable thereon.

A widow is endowed of the third part of all the real estate whereof her husband is seized of an estate of inheritance at any time during the marriage. This interest, termed during the lifetime of her husband *inchoate*, attaches at the instant of marriage to all real estate the husband then owns, and after marriage to all real estate he acquires. Having once attached, it cannot be divested by any act of the husband, or any of his creditors. The wife alone can release it, and she forfeits it only in case of a divorce dissolving the marriage for her misconduct.

The husband cannot either sell or devise his real estate, except subject to this dower right of his wife. The husband's estate by courtesy in his wife's real estate is by no means so broad or so well secured as is the wife's right of dower. It does not attach at all until the birth of a living child, and the wife may absolutely defeat it at any time without any consent on the part of her husband, either by conveying her real estate during her lifetime, or by devising it by her will. It is no longer necessary for the husband to join with the wife in conveying her property.

A husband is liable for necessaries purchased by his wife, and also for money given to the wife by a third person in order to enable her to purchase necessaries, and he is bound to support her and her children without regard to the extent of her individual and separate estate. No similar obligation to furnish necessaries to a husband is imposed upon a wife. The legal definition of necessaries is very broad, being "such things as are actually required for the wife's support commensurate with the husband's means, her wonted living as his spouse, and her station in the community."

In case of a divorce, whether partial or absolute,

obtained by the wife, the husband is required to pay *alimony* for her support during the rest of her life, even if she should re-marry. A wife from whom a husband obtains a divorce cannot be required to contribute in any way to his support.

Although the law has opened wide the door for all women to engage in business, it still discriminates in their favor in many particulars. No woman can be arrested in a civil action, or held by an execution against the body, except in cases in which it is shown that she has committed "a wilful injury to person, character, or property," or has been guilty of such an evasion of duty as is equivalent to a contempt of court. Thus a woman engaged in business cannot be arrested in an action for a debt fraudulently contracted.

All women judgment debtors, whether married or single, enjoy certain exemptions from the sale of their property under execution, which, in the case of men, extend only to a householder; that is, a man who has, and provides for, a household or family.

Every married woman is the joint guardian of her children with her husband, with equal powers, rights, and duties in regard to them with her husband. It is only the survivor, be it father or mother, who possesses the right to appoint a guardian by deed or by will. She has now equal rights with the father over her children.

As matter of practice, the courts when called upon to award the custody of minor children in cases of separation, determine the question with reference solely to the interests of the child, with a strong leaning in the mother's favor.

A husband's creditors have no claim upon the proceeds of a policy of insurance upon his life for the benefit of his wife, unless the annual premiums paid by him shall have exceeded five hundred dollars. The proceeds of such a policy are exempt from execution for any debt owed by the wife.

The statutes contain a large number of special provisions for the benefit of female employees in factories and mercantile houses. In the city of New York, if any man fails to pay the wages due a female employee up to fifty dollars, not only is none of his property exempt from execution, but he is liable to be imprisoned upon a body execution, and kept in close confinement without the privilege of bail. A similar rule is applicable in Brooklyn.

No woman can be called upon to perform military duty.

No woman can be required to serve upon any jury.

No woman can be called upon by the sheriff or any peace officer to assist in quelling a disturbance or making an arrest.

# CHAPTER VI.

The fifth count in the Suffrage Declaration of Sentiments reads as follows : " He has monopolized nearly all the profitable employments, and from those she is permitted to follow she receives but scanty remuneration."

The women who wrote that in 1848, in common with the majority of American women, were presumably being well provided for in their own homes, by men whose boast it was that their wives and daughters did not need or care to seek employment elsewhere. It is true that at that time, because of this supposed advantage, as married women they could not have engaged in separate business that would involve the making of contracts or distinct bargain and sale. To the world the husband was the wife's financial manager. But at that time the wife could enter any of the employments as a paid clerk or worker. This count seems more surprising in view of the fact that, writing only three years later, to a Suffrage convention that met in Akron, Ohio, Mrs. Stanton said : " The trades and professions are all open to us ; let us quietly enter and make

ourselves, if not rich and famous, at least independent and respectable." Two years later still,
Colonel Thomas W. Higginson wrote to another
Suffrage convention that met in Akron, Ohio:
" We complain of the industrial disadvantages of
women, and indicate at the same time their capacities for a greater variety of pursuits. Why not
obtain a statement on as large a scale as possible,
first of what women are doing now, commercially
and mechanically, throughout the Union, and
secondly, of the embarrassments which they meet,
the inequality of their wages, and all the other
peculiarities of their position." This would have
been most valuable and interesting, and it would
seem that something of the kind should have
preceded the sweeping accusation made in the
Declaration; but there appears in their " History "
no evidence of its having been done. In 1859
Caroline H. Dall said, in addressing a Suffrage
convention: " I honor women who act. That is
the reason that I greet so gladly girls like Harriet
Hosmer, Louisa Landor, and Margaret Foley.
Whatever they do, or do not do, for Art, they do
a great deal for the cause of labor. I do not believe any one in this room has an idea of the
avenues that are open to women already." Then
follows a list of the trades then pursued by women
in Great Britain. Of the United States she said:
" Of factory operatives in 1845 there were 55,828
men and 75,710 women. Women are glue-makers,
glove-makers, workers in gold and silver leaf,

hair-weavers, hat and cap-makers, hose-weavers, workers in India-rubber, paper-hangers, physicians, picklers and preservers, saddlers and harness-makers, shoe-makers, soda-room keepers, snuff and cigar-makers, stock and suspender-makers, truss-makers, typers and stereotypers, umbrella-makers, upholsterers, card-makers, photographers, house and sign-painters, fruit-hawkers, button-makers, tobacco-packers, paper-box makers, embroiderers, and fur-sewers." She added: "In New Haven seven women work with seventy men in a clock factory (at half wages)." And in summing up she said: "The great evils that lie at the foundation of depressed wages are that want of respect for labor which prevents ladies from engaging in it, and that want of respect for women which prevents men from valuing properly the work they do. Make women equal with men before the law, and wages will adjust themselves."

Women are equal with men legally and wages have not adjusted themselves, and the law has had no control over the feelings and opinions of men and women. Those who were large-minded enough to respect labor asked no warrant from legislation, and those who were small-minded enough to undervalue woman's work because it was woman's, do so still despite the statutes, and would if women voted at every election. Men were equal with each other before the law, but that did not compel the respect of foolish men, nor did their wages adjust themselves to equality

on that account. If there were more men working in a trade in a given place than the demand
for their products required, the wage would fall,
and so it must with women. But reasons entered
into the market value of woman's work that did
not enter into that of men. Mrs. Dall mentions
but one trade in which the wages were lower for
women, and there they competed with men. Those
seven women working with the seventy men in
New Haven were not expected to be called upon to
support a family by their earnings. If they were
girls, in the natural course of things they were
expected to leave the work whenever they were
ready to marry. If one of them married one of
the seventy men, the firm of employers would
lose her services entirely; but the man who married her would be depended upon to work more
steadily than before, and he would also have more
incentive to do better work in order to command
still higher wages. The long cry of Suffrage has
not been able to bring about "equal pay for equal
work," even where legislation to that effect has
been introduced into Trades Unions and State
laws. This has still rested, and must rest, with
the employer, and his action must be governed by
quality and demand and supply. The attempt
to secure "equal wages" among men has resulted
in bringing down the wages of all to the point of
the poorer workers. The general laws of trade,
like those of government, are based on principles
of universal equity, and however strenuously tem-

porary deviations may be pressed, they return at last to the natural position. This is not saying that there is not great injustice toward labor by capital, and toward capital by labor, but that the foundation principles tend to govern the mutual relations, and forcing that is contrary to these cannot be permanently successful. If the work of women for any reason is unequal, the wages will be, and the mere fact that some particular women work for some particular time the same number of hours, and as well as do the men in the same establishments, does not do away with the fact that women's work in general is not as steady as men's, and is not expected to meet the same emergency of family support. No one can believe more fully than I in equal wages for work that is really equal; but it seems to me that private contract, and not public action, must regulate the matter of special wage.

Government reports show that the average age of the working-girl in this country is but twenty-two years, and that after twenty the number falls off rapidly. Unskilled labor must forever take the place of that which is withdrawn, which is another and most valid reason for lower wages. That lower wages are the result of natural causes, and not of unnatural feeling, is shown in many ways. Woman teachers at the West, where teachers were needed, received as good pay as did men. In New York I heard Superintendent Jasper, I think it was, say: "I am in favor of equal pay for equal work, for the two sexes; but we cannot give it here. We can get twice as many good women teachers as men teachers, and when we need men we must pay at a higher rate." This does not extend to the highest grade of teachers, superintendents, and professors in colleges, where men compete with one another. There the compensation is the same for equal work. In the highest forms of work women compete on equal terms. In literature women are paid, for books or articles, the same prices that men receive. In art this is true. It is the picture or statue or musical ability that counts. Singers receive as much for the soprano as for the tenor voice. Actresses are paid according to " drawing " power, and woman dancers and acrobats, alas! command the highest price.

There is, among others, this fundamental difference between the business life of men and women. For men who pursue occupations outside the home, there are women to manage that home. For women who pursue occupations outside the home, there are, not men, but other women, to manage the home. The final domestic care of the world must come upon women. The final attention to social life must come upon women. In behalf of the women who are constrained, or who choose, to sacrifice their share in this part of the world's necessary work, some other women must do double duty. That this rule has seeming exceptions does not make it less the universal rule.

Nothing, not even "industrial emancipation," is gotten for nothing.

When the count cited above from the Suffrage indictment was written, the factory system had been established in this country twenty-six years. From the Revolution down to 1822, the women of the land had been busy in the homes making the household and personal wear. Sixteen years after the introduction of machinery into Lowell, Mass., 12,507 operatives were at work there, the majority of whom were women, American women and girls. New York State also had its mills. "Fanny Forester" (afterward Mrs. Judson) worked in a mill near her home in that State. She went there, as did hosts of New England girls, Lucy Larcom and Harriet Robinson among the number, to relieve the home, but especially to gain the means of education, for themselves and for their brothers and sisters. The towns afforded better libraries, and there were evening classes that they could attend, things not to be had in the farming districts. In 1850, in twenty-five States, the factory census reported 32,295 men and 62,661 women workers. In 1860 there were 46,-859 men and 75,169 women. Hosiery machinery at this time was giving employment to three times as many women as men. But the emigrant, and not the American man, had been the means of turning out the native woman worker; it was the foreign-born woman who worked for "unequal pay." In 1846, the sewing-machine had been invented. Previous to that time, 61,500 women were employed making boys' clothing by hand for the market, which was twice the number of men so employed, while the woman tailor was as familiar a figure as the dress-maker in every village, where she went from house to house.

In 1861 came our Civil War, with its awful sacrifice of young men. With that also came the heavy money loss, and consequent inability of many men, even where life and limb had been spared, to support their families in the homes. That great conflict, with its stern necessities, its lessons of mutual helpfulness, its military discipline, which taught the value of organization, did more than could ten thousand conventions, even had they been working with knowledge and system, to instruct women in love for work for others. It nerved them to labor for self-support and for the support of those who were now dependent upon them because the strong arm had fallen and the willing heart had ceased to beat. Before the year 1861 had closed, there were a million women in this country earning their daily bread by honorable labor. As time went on, and the slaughter continued, and the nation's debt piled up, and prices became almost fabulous, more and more women asked through blinding tears, "What can I do?" Every trade was thrown open to women, and the laws had placed the married woman where she could compete on equal terms with her unmarried sister, even though

13

she still had the advantage of a husband's support.

A great pother has lately been made by Suffrage workers in New York because a bill was proposed prohibiting married women from teaching in the public schools. This has been the unwritten law in many places for years. The practice was adopted to offset the maintenance of married women. Teachers should receive more pay, but so should poets and artists, and we all hope the time will come when brain work will have more tangible market value.

The sewing-machine had thrown women out of employment, as with it one woman could do the work of many. The number of work-seekers was enlarged by the influx, from the desolated South, of women whose entire living had been swept away. This army of uneducated workers from all sections were compelled not only to compete with men but with themselves as well. They sought, and could seek, only the lighter employments. Suffragists had their wish in regard to man's relinquishment of the "profitable employments," but not in the way they intended. The women for whose sake those profitable employments had been "monopolized" were now not only allowed by law but compelled by circumstance to toil from sun to sun at the best they could find to do; their frailer organizations were forced to bear "the double curse of work and pain." A nobler army of martyrs never turned

their sorrows into blessings by the spirit in which
they met them, than the American women who
put their shoulders to the wheels of business that
were moving in a hundred ways.

In 1843 a humble beginning at industrial education for girls had been made by the Female
Guardian Society. In 1854 Peter Cooper established the Cooper Union with its generous facilities for women in industry and the arts. The
Young Women's Christian Association was
founded in Normal, Illinois, in 1872, and its work
in the industrial branch spread, before many
years, to every city and town in the land. Men
originated for women the first "Woman's Protective Union." In twenty-five years it had
reported legal suits won for 12,000 women, and
$41,000 collected. In 1869 the great organization
of the Knights of Labor was founded, and in its
body of rules was one "to secure for both sexes
equal pay for equal work." Failure proves that
labor cannot, any more than paper, be coined into
money by the mere fiat of a government or an
organization.

But the great impulse to industrial education
came through the Centennial Exposition held at
Philadelphia in 1876. While the land was filled
with the hum of preparation, as their contribution
to that indication of peaceful progress, the Suffrage Associations were rolling up another petition in which to set forth their wrongs. After
General Hawley, manager of the Exposition, had

courteously refused to receive it in a public meeting, it was " pressed upon the Nation's heart " by delegates who pushed their way into Independence Hall.    Outside that historic building, under the broiling sun, with Matilda Joslyn Gage to hold an umbrella over her, Miss Anthony read aloud a " Declaration of Independence " that re-echoed the sentiments of their first Declaration.    It began by saying: " While the nation is buoyant with patriotism, and all hearts are attuned to praise, it is with sorrow we come to strike the one discordant note "—a typical and prophetic sentence.

From 1876 girls, as well as boys, received manual training in the public schools, and when that proved impracticable, the way was found to open industrial schools that should include classes for girls.    Every State, and almost every city and town of any size, had them.    It was not long ere multitudes of societies and organizations furnished means for women's education in business and mechanic arts.    The growth of the philanthropy of self-help is one of the wonders of the past twenty-five years, and women, without the ballot, have largely assisted in developing it.

John Graham Brooks, in a lecture delivered in New York in the winter of 1895–6, on " Some Economic Aspects of the Woman Question," said : " Woman who used to do her work in the house now does it in the factory, and the same work, doing her work under absolutely new and different conditions, a change so great that it closes finally one argument that I hear again and again by those opposed to woman suffrage—namely, that the place for woman is in the home."

One condition under which she works that is not "absolutely new and different" is that of sex. Whatever as a woman she could not do in the home she cannot do abroad as a working-woman. She is in business as a business woman, not as a business man. Economic equality in such things as she can do is as unlike to a similarity in work which ignores sex conditions as a business corporation is to the government under whose laws it exists and by which its rights are defended. But even the external conditions are not so changed as might at first appear. The statistical proof of the youth of the majority of workers, the comparatively small number out of the whole population who go into business, and the fact that the domestic work for these very workers must be done by women, all show this.

The United States Census of 1890 shows that not quite four million women are "engaged in gainful occupations." Of these more than one and a half million are in domestic service, and nearly half a million in professional service, mainly as teachers. The most striking gain has been made in the lighter forms of profitable labor —by stenographers, typewriters, telegraph and telephone operators, cashiers, bookkeepers, etc. In 1870 there were 19,828 of these; in 1890, there were 228,421. The invention of the type-writing

machine appears to be the ballot that has mainly
produced this result.    Carrol D. Wright says that
in twenty cities examined in the United States he
found, among 17,000 working-women, that 15,887
were single, 1,038 were widows, and 745 were
married.    This tells the same story.    The mass of
these women, like the mass of men, are working,
not for public influence or station, but for the own-
ing and holding of a home.    The latest effort in
self-help for the working class is the wise one of
building them good homes.    The best renting property has been found to be that which gives privacy
and those distinctions that mark the family.

The latest report of the New York Bureau of
Statistics of Labor shows that of 8,040 persons
who registered for employment in New York city,
6,458 were men, and 1,582 were women.    Of
these, the foreign-born numbered 4,804, of whom
3,674 were men and 1,140 were women.    The
native-born numbered 3,234, of whom 2,796 were
men, and 442 were women.    The list included
every trade and profession, from that of day
laborer to that of clergyman, from that of school
teacher to that of domestic servant, and showed
that in the city where more women are employed
than in any other place, the proportion of women
to men was less than one fifth, and of native
American to foreign-born women two fifths.

Mr. Brooks would favor suffrage because " in
this new career there are reasons for every whit
of protection."    He mentions, as proof of woman's

changed attitude as an industrial unit, that the Supreme Courts of Illinois and California have decided against special legislation for women. They did so on the ground that " they were now earning their livelihood under men's conditions, and should not have special legislation in business relations." If Mr. Brooks thinks that women wish the ballot to restore the special legislation, he does not know the Suffrage demand for equality. In England, when the laws were under discussion that forbid the employment of women more than a certain number of hours, and of children under certain ages, the Woman Suffrage leaders protested against the former as an infringement of personal rights and the ability to make contracts. But the special legislation for business women goes on, because, after all, the State knows that they are business women, and not business men, and the Suffrage quarrel in regard to privilege *versus* right goes on also.

Before the Committee of the Constitutional Convention, Mrs. Ecob, of Albany, said : " You speak of chivalry. We scorn the word ! What has your chivalry done for the weaker sex ? Women are the upaid laborers of the world—outcasts in government." Mrs. Hood, of Brooklyn, on the same occasion said : " Who dares insult our American manhood by declaring that men will be less courteous to mother, wife, and sister, because they are political equals ? Woman's equality in the industrial world has to-day produced a nobler, better chivalry than was ever conceived by the knights of old."

These two Suffrage leaders will have to settle between themselves the question which they have placed in dispute. It serves to point the moral of dilemma that attends an attempted adjustment of unnatural claims. Meantime government is caring for the weak, and chivalry is doing justice. The Labor Law that went into effect in this State on September 1st provided that children be classified so that those under fourteen years should not be employed in mercantile pursuits. Children between the ages of twelve and fourteen will be permitted to work in vacation, if they can show that they have attended school through the year. The girls between fourteen and twenty-one are not to be allowed to work more than ten hours a day. Their employment before 7 A. M. and after 10 P. M. is forbidden. Women and children are not allowed to work in basements, without permits from the Health Board as to the condition of the basement. Seats are to be provided for woman employees, forty-five minutes given them for luncheon, and proper lunch and toilet rooms to be secured. Penalties, ranging from a fine of $20 for the first offence to imprisonment, are prescribed for violation of the law. In his last report, published in January 1897, the New York Commissioner of Labor considers the low wages and petty wrongs of working women and girls in New York City. He advises the formation of unions among themselves for their better protection.

Mr. Brooks does not agree with those who claim that possession of the ballot would raise wages. Mrs. Ames and Dr. Jacobi think it would only raise them through the indirect influence of the greater respect in which the worker would be held. This is safe ground again, because it is debatable; but the domestic servants of those who hold the former opinion might give them an object-lesson. Unfranchised as the servants are, they have only to make a threat of leaving to secure better wages.

Harriette A. Keyser, who was the special Suffrage champion of the working-woman before the Committee of the Constitutional Convention, gave not one fact or figure to show that the working-woman, where she had the ballot, had already been helped by it, or that it was likely to help her, or how and why it might help her. Among the generalities she uttered was the following: " But the greatest value of the working-woman, to my mind, is that without her economic value this present demand for equal suffrage could never be made. Indeed, the suffrage of the world is due to her. Do I mean by this that every working-woman in the country sees her own value so clearly that she demands enfranchisement ? I could not say this with truth. I make this statement irrespective of what any individual working-woman may think. It is based

upon what she is.  As through the last half century the contention for equal rights has continued,
the working-woman has been the great object-
lesson.  It was not from women of leisure, having
all the rights they want, that inspiration has been
received.  It has been caught from the patient
worker, healing the sick, writing the book, painting the picture, teaching the children, tilling the
soil, working in the factory, serving in the household.  Every stroke of these workers has been
a protest against a disfranchised individuality."
Miss Keyser has mentioned most of the classes in
this country, for, so far as my experience goes,
there is no such thing as a leisure class, in the
sense of an idle class, of women.  Women are
almost universally industrious, and it is a mistake
to suppose that their early industry in the house
was not as much appreciated and counted in the
general fund of work as their more public activity
now.  It is well for Miss Keyser to make her
estimate of the Suffrage value of the working-
woman one that shall have no reference to the
expressed views of the working-woman herself;
because the working-woman seems almost universally not only unconscious of but indifferent to
her attitude as a great object-lesson in favor of
the ballot.  But here is something new.  Suffragists have first claimed that there could be no
working-woman unless there was a ballot in
woman's hand; then they claimed that, although
there was a working-woman despite the fact that

she had not been enfranchised, she was made by the agitation for the ballot ; and now comes Miss Keyser to say that, not only is the working-woman not due to the ballot, or to ballot-seeking, but " the suffrage of the world is due to her," for " without her economic value this present demand for equal suffrage could never have been made!" Tar baby ain't sayin' nuthin'.

Dr. Jacobi, in " Common Sense," says : " Whatever may be the personal privileges of their lot, whatever the legal protection accorded to their earnings, the public status of such a class remains strictly that of aliens. At the present moment this vast and constantly growing army of women industrials constitutes an alien class. The privation for that class of political right to defend its interests is only masked, but not compensated, by its numerous inter-relations with those who have rights." So they are conceded to have personal privileges, and legal protection for earnings. The alienism is then purely political, and works no hardship but what Suffragists conceive to be in the mental attitude of the worker.

Foreign capitalists who own land or plant in the United States are unfranchised. We have large numbers of men working in trades and professions who never have been naturalized, but we do not dream that all these constitute an alien class of industrials. No distinction is made in business opportunity between the voter and non-voter. Neither is any social distinction made regarding worker or employer on account of the relations of either to the ballot. Market value is not measured by suffrage, except in dishonorable transactions, and the women " with ballots in their hands" are not the Government's preferred creditors. The men in the District of Columbia are not conscious of lower wages and industrial ostracism. Again, Dr. Jacobi says: " The share of women in political rights and life—imperfect and deferred during the predominance of militarism—has become natural, has become inevitable, with the advent of industrialism, in which they so largely share."

Industrialism has no more power to change the basis of government than the abolition movement had when certain advocates of it shouted that it was "sinful to vote or hold office, because the government was founded upon physical force and maintained itself by muskets." Industrialism is bringing into this country some of the gravest problems it has ever met. The sympathy of the people is on the side of labor that uses honorable means; but Cleveland and Leadville are among the places that suggest afresh the fact that industrialism must be kept in order for its own sake, for the sake of general peace, and for the sake of its increasing ranks of " alien " women who look to it for " every whit of protection," save that which their own self-respect and that of public opinion can win them.

Again, Dr. Jacobi says: " Notwithstanding the repression of women's civil rights, and their absolute exclusion from even the dream of a political sphere, the women of France engage more freely than anywhere else in business and industry." There is a moral here deeper than can be read at a glance. The first thought suggested is, that industrial success for woman is not in the least dependent upon the vote. The second is, that industrial progress does not command the vote. The third is, that American freedom has worked in the opposite direction from French unstable republicanism. And the fourth is, that industrious France stands appalled at the lack of increase of its population. There are many forces that sap its national life, but perhaps the most conspicuous is the socialistic and anarchistic tendency of its labor organizations. The woman-suffrage idea was first openly proclaimed during the French Revolution. In 1851 the annual Suffrage Convention in this country was called by Paulina Wright Davis, to meet in Worcester, Mass. Ernestine Rose read to the convention two letters addressed to that body through her, written by Jeanne Deroine and Pauline Roland, from a Paris prison. During the revolutionary movements of 1848, these women had played conspicuous rôles. One of them had attempted to nominate the mayor in her native city, the other to be a candidate for the Legislative Assembly. They wrote: "Sisters of America! Your socialist sisters of France are united with you in the vindication of the right of woman to civil and political equality. We have, moreover, the profound conviction that only by the power of association based on solidarity—by the union of the working-classes of both sexes in organized labor, can be acquired, completely and pacifically, the civil and political equality of woman, and the social right for all."

I know the feud, and the grounds for it, between socialism and anarchy. But both are enemies of the social order, and both are favorers of woman suffrage. How "pacifically" the labor movement that originated in France in 1848, and spread throughout Europe, was likely to proceed, we may judge by its constant outbreaks kindred to the recent bomb-throwing in Paris. In the German Working-man's Union, Hasenclever, for many years the leading socialist in the German Reichstag, said: "The Woman Question would be taken by the developed, or, more correctly speaking, the communistic state, under its own control, for in this state" (which was to consist of men and women with equal vote) "when the community bears the obligation of maintaining the children, and no private capital exists, the woman need no longer be chained to one man. The bond between the sexes will be merely a moral one, and if the characters do not harmonize could be dissolved." The "Social Democrat" of Copenhagen has for mottoes: "All men and women over twenty-one should vote." "There should be institutions for the proper bringing up of children." All the communistic and anarchistic labor organizations in Germany, France, Switzerland, Denmark, and England proclaim woman suffrage as a prime factor, and the disruption of the family as its corollary.

There are many who remember the visit to this country of the socialist, Dr. Aveling, and his (so-called) wife, the daughter of Karl Marx. His legal wife had been left in England. Miss Marx said, in reply to the question of a Chicago lady, that love was the only recognized marriage in Socialism, consequently no bonds of any kind would be required. Divorces would be impossible; for when love ceased, separation would naturally ensue.

At a meeting of the Woman's Council held in Washington, in 1888, Mrs. Stanton said: "I have often said to men of the present day that the next generation of women will not stand arguing with you as patiently as we have for half a century. The organizations of labor all over the country are holding out their hands to women. The time is not far distant when, if men do not do justice to women, the women will strike hands with labor, with socialists, with anarchists, and you will have the scenes of the Revolution of France acted over again in this republic."

Mrs. Stanton Blatch, daughter of Elizabeth Cady Stanton, in her lecture in this country two years ago on "The Economic Emancipation of Woman," said that she rejoiced in every co-operative working-woman's dwelling, because it was a blow aimed at the isolated home, and she has just repeated in New York her proposition for the institutional care of children. Alice Hyneman Rhine, in her article on "Woman's Work in America," says of socialistic labor, "It aims to benefit woman by recognizing her as a perfect equal of man, politically and socially; by fixing woman's means of support by the state so as to render her independent of man." "Freedom," a radical socialistic newspaper published in Chicago, where Emma Goldman and her ilk have revealed the true inwardness of such movements, recommends as the first step "equal rights for all, without distinction of race or sex," and the abolition of "class rule." Our most radical socialistic Labor National Convention in New York, this year, had four woman delegates.

The Knights of Labor who first put "equal pay for equal work" into their platform, appeared in their late convention, under the lead of Sovereign, who declared that Gov. Altgeld "was one of the finest types of American manhood to-day." They seem to be drifting toward that phase of Socialism to which Alice Hyneman Rhine referred. There are no greater tyrants than some of the Labor organizations, and one evidence of this is the fact that they prevent the colored man from doing any work outside of a few of the least noble occupations.

With such edged tools as these are our American women playing when they demand, in the name of democracy, in the name of the family, in the name of the working-woman, that the word " sex " shall be inserted in the United States Constitution, and the word " male " be stricken from every State constitution that now contains it.

# CHAPTER VII.

THE sixth count in the Declaration of Sentiments reads: "He closes against her all the
avenues to wealth and distinction which he considers most honorable to himself. As a teacher
of theology, medicine, or law, she is not known."

That statement contains another evidence of
the untruthfulness of a half truth. First, it is an
unwarrantable assumption, of which no proof is
offered, that man had closed against woman any
avenue to wealth and distinction, or that he felt
toward woman the selfish and monopolizing spirit
implied in such accusation. Second, but three of
the avenues, all of which he was said to have
closed against her, are mentioned. Whatever
may be the truth about those three, the no less
honorable, although less arduous, avenues to
wealth and distinction were as open to her as
to him. As educator, author, artist, in painting,
music, and sculpture, she could freely attain to
the same coveted end. The Suffragists did not
decry man's "monopoly" of the honorable and
profitable but severe professions of civil engineering, seamanship, mining engineering, lighthouse

keeping and inspecting, signal service, military and naval duty, and the like. These, and the drudgery of the world's business and commerce, man was welcome to keep.

But, most of all, this Suffrage indictment contains, as do all the rest, another tacit untruth when it assumes that woman's work has not in the past been as honorable to herself and as profitable to the world as has that of man. By setting up a false standard for achievement, and attempting to make everything conform to it, the Suffrage movement has done incalculable harm. It is not progressing to push into an unwonted place merely because it is unwonted, and because you can push in. It is progress to enter it in response both to an inward and an outward need.

When the first Suffrage convention had adopted the Declaration of Sentiments, Lucretia Mott offered a resolution, which was also adopted, declaring that "the speedy success of our cause depends upon the zealous and untiring efforts of men and women for the overthrow of the monopoly of the pulpit, and for the securing to woman an equal participation with men in the various trades, professions, and commerce."

The most remarkable thing about this resolution is, that it was promulgated by a woman who was at that very time a gifted and eloquent preacher, so that to her, who cared for it so highly, man had not closed that avenue to wealth and distinction. As she had a husband to support her

and her children, she was much more free to
attain those desirable ends than most of the ministers who were preaching for humanity's sake
and the gospel's, at salaries ranging from five
hundred to two thousand dollars a year, and who
had families to support out of their slender pit-
tance.  If any woman was in a position to "overthrow the monopoly of the pulpit," surely she
was.  Stately and beautiful of mien, fervent in
spirit, eloquent in language, one who had learned
the Hebrew and Greek that she might read the
Scriptures in the original tongues, what did she
lack?  Not only was no pulpit of another faith
than hers ever opened to her, but more than half
those of her own form of worship were closed
against hearing the inner voice as interpreted by
her.  In that schism that rent the Society of
Friends as no other religious body has ever been
rent, she threw in her fortunes, or led others to
throw in their fortunes (for she had been preaching nine years when the division occurred), with
that portion that placed the " inner light " above
all Scripture.  When the Friends came from the
London meeting to testify against the teachings
of the schismatics, they besought Lucretia Mott to
return to the faith of her childhood, but she
resisted from conviction that she was right.  Elias
Hicks, her leader, had instigated the members of
his congregation to refuse to pay their taxes to
the Government during and following the war of  ·
1812, on the ground that they represented an

encroachment of the secular power on Christian liberty, and were used to support war, which was sin. Lucretia Mott preached that " no Christian can consistently uphold a government based on the sword, or relying on that as an ultimate resort." The country has always suffered from this doctrine. The Tory Quakers of the Revolution called publicly upon Friends " to withstand and refuse to submit " " to instructions and ordinances " not warranted by " that happy Constitution under which we have long enjoyed tranquillity and peace." Thomas Paine, whose parents were Friends, in " The Crisis," says : " The common phrase of these people is, ' Our principles are peace.' To which it may be replied, ' and your practices are the reverse.' " Another striking instance of this disagreement between principle and practice is seen in Lucretia Mott's behavior. From the platform where she demanded the ballot for woman, she proclaimed that all voting was sinful. That bodies of people who so held should continue to enjoy the Government's protection of themselves and their property, through the sacrifices made by those who carried on government by giving willingly their money and their strength, is a proof of our wonderful freedom.

Elizabeth Fry and most of the English Friends would not mention the name of Mrs. Mott. Mrs. Stanton once asked her what she would have done after the Hicksite faction had been voted out of meeting at the World's Conventicle of Friends in

London, if the spirit had moved her to speak when the chairman and members had moved that she be silent, and she answered, "Where the spirit of God is, there is liberty." This is the liberty of anarchy, and it had its due weight in the Suffrage movement. Mrs. Stanton, in the course of a eulogy pronounced at Mrs. Mott's funeral, said: "The 'vagaries' of the Anti-slavery struggle, in which Lucretia Mott took a leading part, have been coined into law; and the 'wild fantasies' of the Abolitionists are now the Thirteenth, Fourteenth, and Fifteenth amendments to the National Constitution. . . . The 'infidel' Hicksite principles that shocked Christendom are now the corner-stones of the liberal religious movement in this country." The vagaries of the Anti-slavery struggle are exactly those that were *not* coined into law. The wild fantasies of the Abolitionists were rejected by those whose sober judgment and steady courage made possible the last constitutional amendments. And no truer is it that the "infidel" Hicksite principles are the corner-stones of any genuine movement of Christian liberality. While the Friends mourn that infidelity and Roman Catholicism have made inroads upon their progress in some places, they have steadily advanced in the other direction from that pointed out by Lucretia Mott. Their educated and paid ministry, their First-day schools, their missions, home and foreign, their music, and simple but set forms, their reports to London of "conversion and profession of faith," and their rapid growth where these things have taken place, all indicate the truth of this. The large meeting at Swartmore College, in the summer of 1896, is another evidence.

The proportion of woman preachers to the different denominations is as follows: The Hicksite-Quakers (as against the orthodox) have the most. So have the German Methodists (United Brethren) as against the orthodox Methodists. The Free-Will Baptists, as against the orthodox Baptists, ordain more woman preachers. The Universalist preceded the Unitarian church in so doing. The Presbyterian and Congregational churches, as a body, have taken no steps in that direction. In the Congregational denomination any separate body of worshippers can ordain whom it sees fit. The Roman Catholic and Episcopal churches have orders which band women as religious workers and remove them more or less from the ordinary life of the world, but they have taken no steps toward ordaining women for the ministry.

We may note that the denominations that have been foremost in building colleges for woman, and in promoting her general advancement in professions and trades, as well as in social and philanthropic matters, are the ones whose pulpits she has not entered. They are also those by which she is most cordially welcomed to speak on all Christian and philanthropic themes. Where her influence is most broadly felt, she has not been taken out of the ordinary life that she was meant to share and to sway. It was from the great denominations that she first crossed the threshold of home to carry home love and principle to foreign countries. In missions she has served in every conceivable form of public benevolence, side by side with man. Real reforms work from within. If the time comes when the other branches of the Christian Church feel as do a few at present, that the exercise of the ministerial office is consistent and appropriate for woman, one that compels no sacrifice of the life and work that are, and must be, peculiarly her own, the ballot will not be needed to place her or to keep her in their pulpits. Whatever may be thought of the profession of the ministry for woman, it must certainly be acknowledged that it is the one farthest removed from political thought and action. If any class of women should be glad to be exempted from the vote, it is the woman preachers.

In her book, "Common Sense," Dr. Jacobi says: "The profession of medicine was thrown open to women when, in 1849, the year following the Revolution, and the passage of the Married Woman's Property Rights Bill, New York State for the first time, at Geneva, conferred a medical diploma on a woman, Elizabeth Blackwell. She was, or rather she became, the sister-in-law of Lucy Stone; and the work of these two women, the one in medicine, the other for equal suffrage, constituted the two necessary halves of one idea."

In 1848, when the first Suffrage convention was

held, twelve women were studying medicine in different parts of the country. Dr. Elizabeth Blackwell was studying that year in Geneva, and when members of the convention wrote to congratulate her, she said, in the course of her reply: "Much has been said of the oppression that woman suffers; man is reproached with being unjust, tyrannical, jealous. I do not so read human life." Dr. Blackwell estimates that within ten years of that time three hundred women had been graduated in medicine. In an address delivered in 1889 before the London Medical School for women in London, Dr. Blackwell said: "I believe that the department of medicine in which the great and beneficent influence of women may be specially exerted is that of the family physician. Not as specialists, but as the trusted guides and wise counsellors in all that concerns the physical welfare of the family, they will find their most congenial field of labor." All this was the exact opposite of the spirit that prevailed in the Association with which Lucy Stone was identified. She declaimed against man's injustice; and when it was proposed, after the civil war had taught the power of organization, to have a constitution and by-laws for the Suffrage movement, Lucy Stone said that she had felt the "thumb-screws and the soul-screws," and did not wish to be placed under them again. "Our duty is merely agitation." After a stormy quarrel, she left to form a new association in New England. Elizabeth Blackwell's name is conspicuous for its absence from Suffrage annals. In the letter referred to she wrote: "The exclusion and constraint woman suffers is not the result of purposed injury or premeditated insult. It has arisen naturally, without violence, because woman has desired nothing more, has not felt the soul too large for the body. But when woman, with matured strength, with steady purpose, presents her lofty claim, all barriers will give way, and man will welcome, with a thrill of joy, the new birth of his sister spirit."

The way in which barriers have fallen, and have been removed by men, in order that woman may enter the noble profession of medicine, is one of the strange stories of this half century. The Civil War, which taught us so much, helped greatly in this. There were some genuine obstacles in the way of woman's education in medicine, and that they were genuine is proved by the fact that, as rapidly as arrangements can be made so that woman can have thorough training by and with her own sex, this is being done. This trend is in opposition to Suffrage action. Dr. Clemence Lozier, who was so long at the head of the Suffrage association in New York City, was the most persistent urger of mixed clinics, and marched in to them at Bellevue, at the head of her classes, defying the delicate instincts of both men and women.

The struggle of the "new" school, which was really as old as Hippocrates, who said four hun-

dred years before Christ that some remedies
acted by the rule of " contraries," and some by
the rule of "similarity," was long and hard compared with that of the entrance of woman upon
the practice of medicine, although the latter
involved sex questions and the former only forms,
and professional prejudice did not die with
woman's adoption of it.

Dr. Jacobi says : " We are perfectly well aware
that industrial and professional competition are
entirely different matters from popular sovereignty. But when we find the same instincts
aroused, the same opposition excited, the same
arguments advanced, and the same determination
manifested, by trades unions, to exclude women
from trades, by learned societies to exclude them
from professions, by universities to exclude them
from learning, and by voters to exclude them from
the polls, we cannot avoid asking whether the
difference in the cases is not balanced by the
identity in the mental attitude of the opponents."
The best trades unions have admitted women to
their protective and wage associations, or, better
still, have helped them to form their own ; the
worst trades unions, the socialistic and anarchistic,
have claimed for them the right to vote. The
learned societies are admitting them profession-
ally as fast as they make themselves worthy.
The men who hold out against their admission to
men's universities are precisely the class of men
who have been most active in assisting to found

for them equal colleges of their own, and they are also the men who are most strenuous against their admission to the polls. In medicine, while co-education is deemed better than ignorance, the tendency is to separate the sexes in study as fast as facilities can be made equal. The opponents of woman's progress and those of woman suffrage are of opposite classes, and their mental attitudes are entirely different. How much harm the struggle for "popular sovereignty" for women has done in hindering the progress of industrial and professional competition, can be judged somewhat by the success of the latter and the failure of the former in the highest fields. It is a significant fact that women do not avail themselves of opportunities open to them in the professions to the extent that it has been claimed they would. The medical examination advertised in January, 1896, by the New York State Civil Service Commission for woman candidates, failed for lack of applicants, although the salaries of women in the State hospitals range from $1,000 to $1,500 a year.

The entrance of woman upon the legal profession raised constitutional questions as to the enactment of law; and so here, as in the matter of the school suffrage, we see how carefully republicanism guarded the post at which must stand the sentinels of liberty. If it might involve law-enforcement, woman could not practise law or vote on the school question; but the Supreme

Court of the United States decided that "the practising of any profession violates no law of the Federal Constitution."

The study of law must prove of great benefit to woman, though here again it has already been shown that it is possible that the greatest practical advantage she will derive from entrance into this noble profession will be from acquiring knowledge of her country's laws, and how to take care of her own property. Widows and unmarried women have almost invariably placed their moneyed interests in the hands of a man, when it would have been better for all concerned that they should have spent some patient thought on the details of their own affairs. The first woman who was admitted to the bar in this State (New York) was a teacher in the Albany Normal College, and she still remains there, and the women's classes for legal study in New York City have been largely composed of those who had no intention of claiming admittance to the bar. That women can and do enter all these professions with credit to themselves, and that they thus enhance the feeling of pride in their sex, which is a strong impulse with women, is matter for profound congratulation, and is evidence that the animus of the Suffrage movement is not that which stirs society.

# CHAPTER VIII.

THE seventh count in the Suffrage indictment declared: " He has denied her facilities for obtaining a thorough education, all colleges being closed against her."

Among the resolutions passed in the first Suffrage convention was one demanding: " Equal rights in the universities," and the first petition presented by Suffrage advocates contained a clause asking that entrance to men's colleges be obtained for women by legal enactment. We note that this is far from being a demand for education for women equal to that given to men in the universities. Men have founded colleges for women, men and women have worked together in securing for woman every facility and opportunity for education of the highest grade; but the "barrier of sex " is not broken down in education. But few of the older colleges for men admit women, and those few, so far as I have learned from conversation with members of their faculties, speak of the arrangement as an experiment, and give the need for economy, combined with a desire to assist women, as a reason for making that experiment. Meantime the knocking at men's literary portals by Suffrage advocates has gone on as vigorously as if women could obtain education in no other way.

In the first Suffrage convention ever held in Massachusetts these two resolutions were adopted: " That political rights acknowledge no sex, and therefore the word 'male' should be stricken from every State constitution ; " and " That every effort to educate woman, until you accord to her her rights, and arouse her conscience by the weight of her responsibilities, is futile, and a waste of labor."

The State in which these sentiments were uttered abounded in fine schools for girls, among which were Mount Holyoke and Wheaton seminaries.

A rapid survey of some of the educational conditions that led to the state of things existing when Suffrage associations were formed, will be in place. Learning seemed incompatible with worship early in the Christian era. The faith that worked by love was " to the Jews a stumbling-block, and to the Greeks foolishness." That great battle between the felt and the comprehended, which in this era we have named the conflict between science and religion, was decided in the mind of the apostle to the Gentiles when he wrote : " We know in part, and we prophesy in part ; when that which is perfect is come, that which is in part shall be done away." He recalled the accusation, " Thou art beside thyself, much learning hath made thee mad," and he hastened to assure the unlettered fishermen and the simple and devout women who were followers of Christ, that "all knowledge" was naught if they had not love; that even faith was vain if it led to the rejection of the diviner wisdom that a little child could understand.

The great learning of Augustine and the Fathers brought into the Church pagan speculations of God and morality, as well as pagan knowledge in art, science, and literature. The Church became corrupted, and a great outcry was made against the learning itself, which was falsely supposed to be the cause of the degeneration of faith. Symonds says that during the Dark Ages that followed upon this first battle between faith and sight, the meaning of Latin words derived from the Greek was lost; that Homer and Virgil were believed to be contemporaries, and "Orestes Tragedia" was supposed to be the name of an author. Milman says that "at the Council of Florence in 1438, the Pope of Rome and the Patriarch of Constantinople, being ignorant, the one of Greek, and the other of Latin, discoursed through an interpreter." It was near the time of the Reformation that a German monk announced in his convent that "a new language, called Greek, had been invented, and a book had been written in it, called the New Testament." "Beware of it," he added, "It is full of daggers and poison."

But the tradition of the love that book revealed had crept into the heart of the world, and now awoke. Through what struggles the "spirit of all truth" promised by Christ was leading, and would lead the world, the history of civilization can tell. Women shared in some degree the outward benefits of the Revival of Learning. They became in not a few instances Doctors of Law and professors of the great universities that sprang up, as well as teachers, transcribers, and illuminators in the great nunneries. I could give a long and honorable list of names of woman writers and artists, in many lands, from Mediæval to modern times; and one of the interesting things revealed by such a record would be the number who were working with, or were directly inspired and helped by, a father or a brother. The Court contained some women who, like Lady Jane Grey, upheld the model of purity while acquiring the learning that naturally accompanied wealth. But elegant letters had again become the associate of moral and religious corruption in the courts, and the "ignorance of preaching" arose to combat it, in Cromwell, the Roundheads, the Dissenters, the Covenanters.

Yet sound learning was not to die that Christian truth might live. Of the band of Pilgrims and Puritans that came first to our shores, about one in thirty was college-bred. While subordinating book-knowledge to piety, they had learned scarcely less the dangers of ignorance. Their

15

first college was founded because of "the dread
of having an illiterate ministry to the churches
when our ministers shall lie in dust." Charles
Francis Adams says, in regard to the establishment of Harvard College : " The records of Harvard University show that, of all the presiding
officers during the century and a half of colonial
days, but two were laymen, and not ministers of
the prevailing denomination." He further says
that " of all who in early times availed themselves
of such advantages as this institution could offer,
nearly half the number did so for the sake of
devoting themselves to the gospel. The prevailing notion of the purpose of education was attended with one remarkable consequence—the
cultivation of the female mind was regarded with
utter indifference."

It was attended with still another remarkable
consequence, the effect of which is felt up to this
hour. Only men who were fitted for a profession
were given a college education. It is well within
my memory when it began to be seriously said:
" A college education is good for a boy, whether
he intends to follow a profession or not ; it will
make him a better business man, or even a better
farmer." The country girl is now, as a rule, better
educated than her brother. It also happened in
those earlier days, that the artist and the musician
were expected to attain knowledge by intuition,
save in technical branches.

The minister was, almost of necessity, like a

magistrate in these semi-religious colonies. The fact of the breaking up into various sects, which we sometimes incline to look upon with regret as defeating Christian unity, really saved the essentials of that unity by preventing the clerical magistrate from establishing a church resting upon state authority. It was obligatory that the civil rulers should be learned, even at the expense of those who carried on the business and the home.

During the first two hundred years of our existence it would have been almost absurd to expect that women would be extensively educated outside the home. The country was poor, and struggling with new conditions, and great financial crises swept over it. There were wars and rumors of wars. Until after 1812–15 American independence was not an assured fact. Whatever may be said of the present, woman's place in America then was in the home, and nobly did she fill that place. That she had not been wholly uninstructed in even elegant learning, is evidenced by the share she took in literature and in the discussion of religious and public matters, and in such personal records as that of Elder Faunce, who eulogized Alice Southworth Bradford for " her exertions in promoting the literary improvement and the deportment of the rising generation." Dame schools were early established for girls, and here were often found the sons of the farmer and the mechanic. These were established in Massachusetts in 1635. Late in 1700, girls were admitted through the summer to "Latin schools" where boys were taught in winter, and in 1789 women began to be associated with men as teachers. In 1771 Connecticut founded a system of free schools in which boys and girls were taught. In 1794 the Moravians founded a school for girls at Bethlehem, Pennsylvania. Here were educated the sisters of Peter Cooper, the mother of President Arthur, and many women who became exponents of culture.

New England began before this to have fine private schools for girls, but no great step was taken until Miss Hart (afterward Mrs. Willard) had become so successful with her academy teaching in her native town of Berlin, Connecticut, and in Hartford, that three States simultaneously invited her to establish schools within their borders. She went to Massachusetts, but afterward, at the solicitation of Governor Clinton, of New York, she removed her school to Troy, in 1821. It was a new departure, and there was ignorant prejudice to overcome. Governor Clinton, in an appeal to the legislature for aid, said : "I trust you will not be deterred by commonplace ridicule from extending your munificence to this meritorious institution." They were not deterred. An act was passed for the incorporation of the proposed institute, and another which gave to female academies a share of the literary fund. The citizens of Troy contributed liberally, and the success of an effort in woman's high education was assured.

As early as 1697 the Penn Charter School was founded, and it has lived until to-day. Provision was made " at the cost of the people called Quakers," for "all children and servants, male and female, the rich to be instructed at reasonable rates, the poor to be maintained and schooled for nothing." They also provided for " instruction for both sexes in reading, writing, work, languages, arts and sciences." The boys and girls have been taught separately, the girls' school being much behind the boys', neither Latin nor other ancient language forming a part of their curriculum. Friends are just beginning to discuss giving higher education to girls. This is a fact especially significant in our discussion, because it has always been claimed that the Quaker doctrine that "souls have no sex " led them to place woman on an " equality" with man before other sects had thought of allowing that they were equals. Lucretia Mott, Susan Anthony, Abby Kelley, and a great body of the women who adopted the resolution that set forth the uselessness of educating woman until she could vote, and who clamored for her entrance to men's institutions, were all of this sect that has kept its women generally far behind in the acquisition of knowledge.

In 1845 Mrs. Willard was invited to address the Teachers' Convention that met in Syracuse. She prepared a paper in which she set forth the idea that, " women, now sufficiently educated, should be employed and furnished by the men as com-

mittees, charged with the minute cares and supervision of the public schools," but declined the
honor tendered her of delivering it in person.
Sixty gentlemen from the convention visited her
at the hotel, and, at their earnest request, she read
the essay, which met with their emphatic approval
of the plan she proposed. The employment of
women in the common schools, and the system of
normal schools, were projected by her.

A Teachers' Convention was held in Rochester
in 1852. Miss Anthony, though a teacher, was
not in attendance upon it, but she records that she
went in and listened for a few hours to a discussion of the causes that led to their profession being held in less esteem than those of the doctor,
lawyer, and minister. In her judgment, the kernel of the matter was not alluded to, so she arose
and said: "Mr. President." She records that " at
length President Davies stepped to the front and
said in a tremulous, mocking tone, "What will
the lady have?" " I wish, sir," she said, " to speak
to the question." "What is the pleasure of the
convention?" asked Mr. Davies. A gentleman
moved that she be heard; another seconded the
motion; whereupon, she records, " a discussion,
pro and con, followed, lasting full half an hour,
when a vote was taken of the men only, and per-
mission was granted by a small majority." She
adds that it was lucky for her that the thousand
women crowding that hall could not vote on the
question, for they would have given a solid "No."

The president then announced "The lady can speak." "It seems to me, gentlemen," said she, "that none of you quite comprehend the cause of the disrespect of which you complain. Do you not see that, so long as society says a woman is incompetent to be a lawyer, minister, or doctor, but has ample ability to be a teacher, every man of you who chooses this profession tacitly acknowledges that he has no more brains than a woman? Would you exalt your profession, exalt those who labor with you. Would you make it more lucrative, increase the salaries of the women engaged in the noble work of educating our future Presidents, Senators, and Congressmen."

Several thoughts arise in regard to this scene, which was so strongly in contrast with the conduct of Mrs. Willard or any of the great educators. Miss Anthony gave no reason for her belief that the entrance of woman upon the other professions would raise either the status or the wages of those engaged in the teacher's profession, and as a matter of fact they have not done so. It was not the society that cast scorn at woman's "lack of brains" which assisted to remove the natural prejudice against her assuming duties that had been deemed unsuited to her physique and her necessary work.

Meantime, one year before the Rochester meeting was held, the first college for women had been chartered at Auburn, New York, under the name of "Auburn Female University." In 1853 it was transferred to Elmira, and it was formally opened in 1855. It was placed under the care of the Congregational Church, but its charter required that it should have representative trustees from five other denominations. Its course of study for the degree of A. B. was essentially the same that was then pursued in the men's colleges of the State. It was expected to rely upon endowment, which put woman's education upon a new and more secure footing.

Suffrage leaders lose no opportunity to represent the Church as an enemy to woman's advancement. Nothing can be further from the truth; and in striking evidence stand the colleges, which, while unsectarian in spirit and in method, have been established and cared for by special religious denominations. Dr. Jacobi, in her book " Common Sense," takes up the tale and says : "The Mount Holyoke Seminary, the immediate successor of that at Troy, was opened in 1837 by Miss Lyon, in spite of the opposition of the clergy." Many besides the clergy were opposed to the plan for which Miss Lyon was endeavoring to raise money. Her idea that the entire domestic work of the establishment could be done by pupils and teachers, was thought unwise and hopeless. In that noble school, where thousands of women have been educated, a great number have become missionaries. When a Suffrage convention in session in Worcester wrote to Miss Lyon, asking her to interest herself in the wrongs of her sex, she answered, " I cannot leave my work." Neither was Vassar College founded from any impulse or suggestion of Suffrage agitators, but in a spirit exactly the opposite. The real impetus to its founding came from Milo Parker Jewett, who was born in Vermont in 1808, and was graduated at Dartmouth College and at Andover Theological Seminary. He was active in the formation of the common-school system of Ohio, and in 1839 he founded The Judson Female Institute in Marion, Alabama. He established a seminary for girls in Poughkeepsie in 1855. He had studied law, and became the friend and legal adviser of Matthew Vassar, who, being unmarried, was casting about for a method of disposing of his fortune. He suggested to Mr. Vassar an endowed college for women, and visited the universities and libraries of Europe with a plan of organization in mind. Mr. Vassar gladly accepted this great enlargement upon an idea that had lain dormant in his own mind, and Vassar College was founded, Dr. Jewett becoming its first president in 1862.

I may claim to have been beside the cradle of Vassar College; for when Dr. Jewett resigned the presidency in 1864, my father named the successor who was appointed, Dr. John H. Raymond, his life-long friend. Dr. Raymond came to Rochester to discuss a plan of work, and, knowing my father's interest, I was on tiptoe to hear about the new college. At my earnest solicitation, he and Dr. Raymond and Prest. Anderson

permitted me to be present at their discussions.
I learned to comprehend the value of womanliness
to the world by the estimate that those noble
educators put upon it. It was evident that they
were arranging for those for whose minds they
felt respect. They made no foolish remarks
about the superiority, inferiority, or equality of
the sexes, and had no contempt to throw upon
the old education of tutor, and library, and young
ladies' seminary. They did not sneer at the
" female mind," but they did talk of the feminine
mind as of something as distinct in its essence
from the masculine mind as the feminine form
is distinct in its outlines. To " preserve womanliness" was a task they felt they must fulfil,
or the women for whose good they labored would
one day call them to account. The dictum so frequently in the mouths of Suffrage leaders, " There
is no sex in brain," would have been abhorrent
to them. In their view, there was as much sex in
brain as in hand ; and the education that did not,
through cultivation, emphasize that fact, would
be a lower and not a higher product. They
laid that intellectual corner-stone in love, and in
the faith that the same womanly spirit which,
when there was not college education enough to
go round, had said, " Give it to the boys, because
their work must be public," would find, through
the glad return the boys were making, a way to
teach the world still higher lessons of womanly
character and influence. Since that time, college

after college has arisen without a dream on the part of the founders, faculties, or students that "every effort to educate woman, until you accord to her the right to vote, is futile and a waste of labor," and it may well be that the women educated in these colleges will decide that, because political rights do acknowledge sex, therefore the word "male" should not be stricken from any State constitution.

Before the committee of the New York State Constitutional Convention in 1894, Mr. Edward Lauterbach, who was arguing in favor of woman suffrage, said : " It was only after the establishment of the Willard School at Troy, only after its noble founder, believing that women and men were formed in the same mould, successfully tried the experiment of educating women in the higher branches, that steps for higher education became generally taken." If Mr. Lauterbach imagines that Mrs. Willard was in the most distant way an advocate of woman's doing the same work as man in the same way, he is unfamiliar with her life and work. Mrs. Willard, in setting forth her ideal of woman's education, said " Education should be adapted to female character and duties. To do this would raise the character of man. . . . Why may not housewifery be reduced to a system as well as the other arts ? If women were properly fitted for instruction, they would be likely to teach children better than the other sex; they could afford to do it cheaper; and men

might be at liberty to add to the wealth of the
nation by any of the thousand occupations from
which women are necessarily debarred." Old-
fashioned wisdom, but choicely good. Mr. Lauterbach further said : "What wonder that, being
so fully equipped in every mental attribute, in
every intellectual qualification, they will be able
not only to cast a vote but to take practical part
in the administration of the government?"

A female Solon would be a woman still, and
in a democracy the intellectual is not the only
qualification needed. This certainly was the
belief of Mrs. Willard, and in 1868, when the
Suffrage leaders were holding a convention in
Washington, and were urging that Congress
should pass a sixteenth amendment admitting
women to suffrage, Almira Lincoln Phelps, sister
of Mrs. Willard, herself an educator and an
author of text-books, wrote to Isabella Beecher
Hooker : "Hoping you will receive kindly what
I am about to write, I will proceed without
apologies. I have confidence in your nobleness
of soul, and that you know enough of me to
believe in my devotion to the best interests of
woman. I can scarcely realize that you are giving
your name and influence to a cause which, with
some good, but, as I think, misguided women,
numbers among its advocates others with loose
morals. . . . If we could with propriety petition
the Almighty to change the condition of the
sexes, and let men take a turn in bearing chil-

dren and in suffering the physical ailments peculiar to women, which render them unfit for certain
positions and business, why, in this case, if we
really wish to be men, and thought God would
change the established order, we might make our
petition ; but why ask Congress to make us men ?
Circumstances drew me from the quiet domestic
life while I was yet young, but success in
labors which involved publicity, and which may ·
have been of advantage to society, was never
considered as an equivalent to my own heart
for such a loss of retirement. In the name of my
sainted sister, Emma Willard, and of my friend
Lydia Sigourney, and, I think I might say, in the
name of the women of the past generation who
have been prominent as writers and educators
(the exception may be made of Mary Wollstonecraft, Frances Wright, and a few licentious
French writers) in our own country and in Europe,
let me urge the high-souled and honorable of our
sex to turn their energies into that channel which
will enable them to act for the true interests of
their sex."

In a woman's club, last winter, a New York
teacher, Miss Helen Dawes Brown, a graduate of
Vassar College, founder of the Woman's University Club and also one of the founders of Bar-
nard College, in a speech said in part : " The
young girl who doesn't dance, who doesn't play
games, who can't skate and can't row, is a girl to
be pitied. She is losing a large part of what

Chesterfield calls the 'joy and titivation of youth.' If our young girl has learned to be good, teach her not to disregard the externals of goodness. Let our girls, in college and out, learn to be agreeable. A girl's education should, first of all, be directed to fitting her for the things of home. We talk of woman as if the only domestic relations were those of wife and mother. Let us not forget that she is also a granddaughter, a daughter, a sister, an aunt. I should like to see her made her best in all these characters, before she undertakes public duties. The best organization in the world is the home. Whatever in the education of girls draws them away from that, is an injury to civilization."

At the close of an article in the "Outlook," written by Elizabeth Fisher Read, of Smith College, she said, speaking of their last adaptation of athletics: "From the beginning, the policy of Smith College has been, not to duplicate the means of development offered in men's colleges, but to provide courses and methods of study that should do for women what the men's courses did for them. Emphasis has been put, not on the resemblances between men and women, but rather on the differences. The effort has not been to turn out new women, capable of doing anything man can do, from walking thirty miles to solving the problems of higher mathematics. Instead of this, the college has tried to develop its students along natural womanly lines, not along the lines that would naturally be followed in training men."

This sounds strangely like Mrs. Willard, who would be the first to rejoice in the new education and in the old spirit that it can develop. Of course Suffrage claims to have the same end in view. Every college woman must decide for herself where she will stand on the question. So far, there never has been any open affiliation between the colleges and the Suffrage movement. We wait to hear a final verdict.

A contributor to the Suffrage department of the Woman's Edition of the Rochester " Post-Express," March 26, 1896, said : " Will Rochester give to its daughters the same advantages as to its sons, or will it say to the girls who have no money to leave home and seek in Smith and Wellesley the culture they cannot procure here : ' You cannot be thoroughly educated; you have no money ; you can have no education ; sit and spin ; bake and brew—but don't bother about higher education,' or will the University of Rochester recognize the one splendid opportunity that awaits it, the one last chance to take its proper place and become all that the highest American standards demand for a University ? "

The time has not yet fully come when these same sentimentalists shall say to the faculty and trustees of Vassar, Wellesley and Smith : " Will you not give to the boys of Poughkeepsie, North-hampton, and Wellesley the same advantages as to the girls? Or will you say to them: 'You cannot be thoroughly educated; you have no money; you can have no education; work in the shop or on the farm, but don't bother about higher education.'" This is Suffrage logic, and there is no more reason why the educational institutions in which men study from the age of eighteen to twenty-two should be invaded by women of that age, than why women's institutions should be invaded by men. Yet this would be the destruction of our women's colleges. When Miss Anthony headed a delegation that went bodily to force co-education on Rochester University, she was told that classes open to women had been connected with the college for years.

The kind of education best suited to the idea of Suffrage is a training in political history and present political issues; but the women who have talked loudly and vaguely of the right of suffrage for years have been the last to present such knowledge. I have read their "History," attended their conventions, glanced at their magazines, but never have come upon the discussion of a single public issue. I think those most familiar with it will bear me out if I make the statement that their principal periodical, "The Woman's Journal," edited by Mary A. Livermore, Julia Ward Howe, Mr. Blackwell, and Alice Stone Blackwell, has not contained any presentations of questions of public policy in the past ten years.

Those whose names are signed to the Suffrage

Woman's Bible, and who are therefore respon-
sible for that disgraceful effusion, have little right
to claim to be intelligent instructors of their sex.
With an ignorance that is monumental, Frances
Ellen Burr glories in the fact that "the Revising
Committee refer to a woman's translation of the
Bible as their ultimate authority for the Greek,
Latin, and Hebrew text," and they add that
"Julia Smith, this distinguished scholar," is the
only person, man or woman, who ever made a
translation of the Bible without help. They say:
"Wycliff made a translation from the Vulgate assisted by Nicholas of Hereford. He was not sufficiently familar with Hebrew and Greek to translate
from those tongues. Coverdale's translation was
not done alone. Tyndale, in his translation, had
the assistance of Frye, of William Roye, and also
of Miles Coverdale. Julia Smith translated the
whole Bible absolutely alone, without consultation
with any one"! Again they say, "King James
appointed fifty-four men of learning to translate
the Bible. Seven of them died, and forty-seven
carried the work on. Compare this corps of
workers with one little woman performing the
Herculean task without one suggestion or word
of advice from mortal man"! Yes, compare it!
Uncultured Julia Smith, stirred by the Millerite
prophecies, did the best she could to enlighten
her own mind, and should be honored for so
doing; but what is to be said of the women who
in this day, in cool print, are willing to show that

16

they have no comprehension of her grotesque errors or of the difficulties that beset a real scholar in his noble task ?  Protest at woman's educational deprivation comes with ill-grace from those who have thus revealed their own lack of knowledge of the oldest literature in the world, the model of poetry and prose, the guardian of the purity of our English speech.

Educated women desire that woman should do all that strength and time allow in the care of the public schools.   The school suffrage ought to be a boon for them.   But it does not, so far, look as if women could make it so.   The figures of the school vote of women in Connecticut, for three years, occasion serious question whether the use of the ballot is the way in which woman is to effect anything.   In Staten Island, ignorance in women voted out education, and a tremendous effort had to be made to vote it in again.   The number of men who voted at the last general election in Connecticut was about 164,000.   The women outnumber the men, but the following table represents the school vote in the State of Emma Willard.   It certainly does not represent the amount of interest taken in education, nor in the common schools :

| COUNTIES. | 1893. | 1894. | 1895. |
|---|---|---|---|
| Hartford | 1293 | 1186 | 689 |
| New Haven | 973 | 949 | 570 |
| New London | 364 | 373 | 185 |
| Fairfield | 273 | 198 | 126 |

| COUNTIES. | 1893. | 1894. | 1895. |
|---|---|---|---|
| Windham .................. | 176 | 182 | 148 |
| Litchfield .................. | 159 | 85 | 50 |
| Middlesex.................. | 60 | 136 | 101 |
| Tolland ................... | 372 | 137 | 37 |

This gives the results from all but three or four towns in the State. Aside from any other considerations, the uncertainty attending the vote of an element whose first call is elsewhere than at the polls, is a menace to the welfare of the schools as well as of republican institutions.

One of the grievances of the Suffrage leaders lay in the fact that the literary women of the country would express no sympathy with their efforts. Poets and authors in general were denounced. Gail Hamilton, who had the good of woman in her heart, who was better informed on public affairs than perhaps any woman in the United States, and whose trenchant pen cut deep and spared not, always reprobated the cause. Mrs. Stowe stood aloof, and so did Catherine Beecher, though urged to the contrary course by Henry Ward Beecher and Isabella Beecher Hooker. In a letter to Mrs. Cutler, Catherine Beecher said: "I am not opposed to women's speaking in public to any who are willing to hear, nor am I opposed to women's preaching, sanctioned as it is by a prophetic apostle—as one of the millennial results. Nor am I opposed to a woman's earning her own independence in any lawful calling, and wish many more were open to her which are now closed. Nor am I opposed to the organization and agitation of women, as women, to set forth the wrongs suffered by great multitudes of our sex, which are multiform and most humiliating. Nor am I opposed to women's undertaking to govern boys and men—they always have, and they always will. Nor am I opposed to the claim that women have equal rights with men. I rather claim that they have the sacred superior rights that God and good men accord to the weak and defenceless, by which they have the easiest work, the most safe and comfortable places, and the largest share of all the most agreeable and desirable enjoyments of this life. My main objection to the Woman-Suffrage organization is this, that a wrong mode is employed to gain a right object. The right object sought is, to remedy the wrongs and relieve the sufferings of great multitudes of our sex; the wrong mode is that which aims to enforce by law instead of by love. It is one which assumes that man is the author and abettor of all these wrongs, and that he must be restrained and regulated by constitutions and laws, as the chief and most trustworthy methods. I hold that the fault is as much, or more, with women than with men, inasmuch as we have all the power we need to remedy the wrongs complained of, and yet we do not use it for that end. It is my deep conviction that all reasonable and conscientious men of our age, and especially of our country, are not only willing but anxious to provide for the good of our sex. They will gladly bestow all that is just, reasonable, and kind, whenever we unite in asking in the proper spirit and manner. In the half a century since I began to work for the education and relief of my sex, I have succeeded so largely by first convincing intelligent and benevolent women that what I aimed at was right and desirable, and then securing their influence with their fathers, brothers, and husbands, and always with success. Why not take the shorter course, and ask to have the men do for us what we might do for ourselves if we had the ballot ? Now if women are all made voters, it will be their duty to vote, and also to qualify themselves for that duty. But already women have more than they can do well in all that appropriately belongs to them, and, to add the civil and political duties of men, would be deemed a measure of injustice and oppression by those who are opposed."

Miss Beecher, like Mrs. Willard and Mrs. Phelps, made text-books for the use of her own seminaries, and her Arithmetic, and Mental and Moral Philosophy, and Applied Theology, were among the educational forces of her day. It is one of the significant signs of the times that science and education, as well as philanthropy, are occupying themselves just now with childhood and motherhood and housewifery. Mrs. Willard's high ideal of womanliness is beginning to be set forth by the electric light of modern thought.

# CHAPTER IX.

THE eighth count in the Suffrage indictment reads : " He allows her in Church, as well as in State, but a subordinate position, claiming Apostolic authority for her exclusion from the ministry, and, with some exceptions, from any public participation in the affairs of the Church."

More than thirty years later than this, Mrs. Stanton, Miss Anthony, and Mrs. Gage wrote in the preface to their " History of Woman Suffrage :" " American men may quiet their consciences with the delusion that no such injustice exists in this country as in Eastern nations. Though, with the general improvement in our institutions, woman's condition must inevitably have improved also, yet the same principle that degrades her in Turkey insults her here. Custom forbids a woman there to enter a mosque, or call the hour for prayers ; here it forbids her a voice in Church councils or State legislatures. . . . The Church, too, took alarm, knowing that with the freedom and education acquired in becoming a component part of the Government, woman would not only outgrow the power of the priesthood, and religious

246

superstitions, but would also invade the pulpit, interpret the Bible anew from her own standpoint, and claim an equal voice in all ecclesiastical councils. With fierce warnings and denunciations from the pulpit, and false interpretations of Scripture, women have been intimidated and misled, and their religious feelings have been played upon for their more complete subjugation. While the general principles of the Bible are in favor of the most enlarged freedom and equality of the race, isolated texts have been used to block the wheels of progress in all periods; thus bigots have defended capital punishment, intemperance, slavery, polygamy, and the subjection of woman. The creeds of all nations make obedience to man the corner-stone of her religious character. Fortunately, however, more liberal minds are now giving us higher and purer expositions of the Scriptures."

It is fifteen years since these statements were made, and we have now the first instalment of " the Bible interpreted anew from her own standpoint," which presumably issues, in their view, from more liberal minds, and is higher and purer than the old one. In the Introduction to that Suffrage Woman's Bible (which is as yet only a commentary on the Pentateuch), Mrs. Stanton says: " From the inauguration of the movement for woman's emancipation the Bible has been used to hold her in her ' divinely appointed sphere ' prescribed by the Old and New Testaments.

The canon and civil law, Church and State, priests and legislators, all political parties and religious denominations, have alike taught that woman was made after man, of man, and for man,—an inferior being, subject to man. Creeds, codes, Scriptures, and statutes are all based on this idea. The fashions, forms, ceremonies, and customs of society, church ordinances, and discipline, all grow out of this idea. . . . So perverted is the religious element in her nature, that with faith and works she is the chief support of the Church and Clergy,—the very powers that make her emancipation impossible."

I know that many believers in Suffrage are also believers in the Bible and in denominational Christianity. Mrs. Helen Montgomery says, in the Woman's edition of the Rochester " Post-Express," that one reason for her favorable consideration of it is, that " Two-thirds of the membership of the Christian church cannot express their conviction at the polls, since women may not vote." " Much of the callousness of politicians to church opinion," she adds, " comes from the knowledge that that opinion is backed by few votes." I also know that many of those who disbelieve in Suffrage may also disbelieve in the Bible, the clergy, and the Church. I further recognize the fact that the church and religion are not synonymous terms. I have no attacks to make, and no special pleading to do. I am discussing the question of Suffrage as I find it in the writing and the speech of its proposers and its present conspicuous advocates. Each American woman has this mighty problem before her, and she must settle it according to her own conscience and best enlightenment.

Mrs. Stanton admits with shame that woman is one of the chief supporters of the Church. Mrs. Montgomery says with delight that she forms two-thirds of the Christian Church. Individual members of Suffrage organizations may be in sympathy with Christianity, or against it; but the movement itself cannot be on both sides of this question. What is its record? I will endeavor to trace it, and will then, as best I may, attempt to say a few words upon the general subject of the " subordination of woman."

In the course of the first clause of their accusation, the women say: " Claiming Apostolic authority for her exclusion from the ministry." In view of the fact that Paul frequently alludes to the teaching and ministrations of women, it has come to be generally thought among Christian scholars, I believe, that this injunction that they " keep silence in the churches," referred to the propriety of their conduct in the moral,—or rather the immoral,—atmosphere by which the Church at Corinth was surrounded. This seems reasonable, because it may be observed that, in writing to Timothy, who was in Macedonia, to Titus, who was in Crete, and to the Church at Ephesus, while he repeats his general injunctions of woman's submission to man, and especially to her husband, he says nothing relative to her public work in the church. But if Paul had been writing to the church in New England, in 1634, and in New York in 1774, his injunction to silence might well have been applied to the first woman preachers to whom Americans were called upon to listen. When Anne Hutchinson, in Boston, preached that "the power of the Holy Spirit dwelleth perfectly in every believer, and the inward revelations of her own spirit, and the conscious judgment of her own mind are of authority paramount to any word of God," she shook the young colony to its foundation, as no man had shaken it. The militia that had been ordered to the Pequot war refused to march, because she had proclaimed their chaplain to be "under a covenant of works, and not under a covenant of grace." Her influence, and not her ballot, if she had one, threatened anarchy in the state, and caused a schism in the church such as might have crushed out the life from the infant body to which Paul was writing.

· In 1774 appeared the next public woman preacher, Ann Lee. She proclaimed that God was revealed a dual being, male and female, to the Jews; that Jesus revealed to the world God as a Father; and that she,—Ann Lee, "Mother Ann,"—was God's revelation of the Mother, "the bearing spirit of the creation of God." She founded the sect of Shakers, whose main articles of belief, besides the one above mentioned, were :

community of goods; non-resistance to force, even
in self-defence; the sinfulness of all human authority, and consequently the sinfulness of participation in any form of government; absolute
separation of the sexes, and consequently no marriage institution. Her mission as "the Christ of
the Second Appearing," began with her announcement of God's wrath upon all marriage, and
the public renunciation of her own. In New
York, as in New England, her proclamations
against government and war tended directly to
anarchy, and in the momentous year 1776 she
was for that reason imprisoned in Poughkeepsie,
whence she was released by Governor Clinton's
pardon.

The next pulpitless preacher, in the succession
we are considering, appeared in this country in
1828. Her name was Frances Wright. She was
a person of totally different mind and methods
from Anne Hutchinson and Ann Lee. She was
professedly an enemy of religion. Anne Hutchinson attacked church and state in the name of
Christian human perfection. Ann Lee attacked
church and state in the name of woman; she
preached communism and separation of the sexes
in the name of Christ; she taught the abolition of
marriage. Frances Wright preached communism
and sex license in the name of irreligion. In
opening the columns of the " Free Inquirer " to
discussion, in New York, in 1828, she said: "Religion is true—and in that case the conviction of

its truth should dictate every human word and
govern every sublunary action,—or it is a deception. If it is a deception, it is not useless only, it
is mischievous; it is mischievous by its idle ter-
rors; it is mischievous by its false morality; it is
mischievous by its hypocrisy; by its fanaticism;
by its dogmatism; by its threats; by its hopes;
by its promises; and last, though not least, by its
waste of public time and public money." While
deciding that it was a deception, she revealed
the evil results to which abandonment of all faith
can lead a woman with a clever brain and a fear-
less tongue. She constantly denounced religion
as the source of all injustice and bigotry and of
the "enslavement of women."

The editors of the "Suffrage History" say: "As
early as 1828 the standard of the Christian party
in politics was openly unfurled. Frances Wright
had long been aware of its insidious efforts, and
its reliance upon women for its support. Ignorant,
superstitious, devout, woman's general lack of
education made her a fitting instrument for the
work of thus undermining the republic. Having
deprived her of her just rights, the country was
now to find in woman its most dangerous foe.
Frances Wright lectured that winter in the large
cities of the western and middle States, striving to
rouse the nation to the new danger which threatened it. The clergy at once became her most
bitter opponents. The cry of 'infidel' was started
on every side, though her work was of vital im-

portance to the country and undertaken from the purest philanthropy."

It was high time that a Christian and a non-Christian party in politics should unfurl a banner; for to the dauntless courage of the land from which she came—Scotland—she added the polished manner of the country from which came D'Arusmont, the husband from whom she was soon parted. To the zeal of the Covenanter, the moral blackness of the infidel, and the political creed of the Commune, she united the doctrine of Free Love. As she set these forth with blandishments of speech and manner, the country did indeed find in this woman a most dangerous foe. When "Fanny Wright societies" sprang up in New York and the West, horror might well be felt by lovers of the Republic.

Lucretia Mott was the next public preacher in this succession. Pure in personal character, lofty in spirit, winning in address, she took for her motto, "Truth for Authority, not Authority for Truth." As authority for that truth, she took Elias Hicks.

Dr. Jacobi, in "Common Sense," says: "The abolitionists were declared to have set aside the laws of God when they allowed women to speak in public: and, by a pastoral letter, the Congregational churches of Massachusetts were directed to defend themselves against heresy, by closing their doors to the innovators. The Methodists denounced the Garrisonian societies as no-government, no-Sabbath, no-church, no-Bible, no-marriage, women's rights societies." Not the Methodists alone, but the Congregationalists, the Presbyterians, the Episcopalians, the Baptists, the Unitarians, the Universalists, and the Quakers so denounced that faction of them in which culminated many of the doctrines of Anne Hutchinson, Ann Lee, Frances Wright, and Lucretia Mott.

In an appeal to the women of New York, in 1860, signed by Elizabeth Cady Stanton, Lydia Mott, Ernestine Rose, Martha C. Wright, and Susan B. Anthony, we read : "The religion of our day teaches that, in the most sacred relations of the race, the woman must ever be subject to the man; that in the husband centres all power and learning; that the difference in position between husband and wife is as vast as that between Christ and the Church; and woman struggles to hold the noble impulses of her nature in abeyance to opinions uttered by a Jewish teacher, which, alas! the mass believe to be the will of God."

In 1895, among the names of those responsible for the Suffrage Woman's Bible, we find three to which the title "Rev." is prefixed. The opening commentary on the first verses of Genesis, where the creation of man is described, says : " Instead of three male personages, as generally represented, a Heavenly Father, Mother, and Son would seem more rational. The first step in the elevation of woman to her true position, as an equal factor in

human progress, is the cultivation of the religious
sentiment in regard to her dignity and equality,
the recognition by the rising generation of an ideal
Heavenly Mother, to whom their prayers should
be addressed, as well as to a Father." Here is
Ann Lee's doctrine revived with a mocking suggestion that savors more of Frances Wright than
of its poor, half-crazed author. The soul-suffi-
ciency of Ann Hutchinson, the spiritual anarchy
of Lucretia Mott, the infidelity and the veiled
coarseness of Frances Wright, have all found fit
setting in this commentary on the Pentateuch. I
know that Miss Anthony repudiates the Suffrage
Woman's Bible in the name of the Association of
which she is President. It certainly does not
represent the faith or the culture or the doctrines
of many who belong to that body; but she cannot really repudiate it for herself or for them. It
was promised in the History of which she is co-
editor, it was foreshadowed in her circular quoted
above, as well as in innumerable speeches of hers
in convention. Those Christian and philanthropic
bodies that have attached themselves to the Suffrage movement have this book to account for
and with. Whatever they may personally decide
to think or say of it, it is the consummate blossom
of the spirit of the Suffrage movement, and the
names it bears upon its title-page represent the
varied classes that have worked for the political
enfranchisement of woman. By the world outside it will so be dealt with.

Few movements have been started, especially among women, that did not professedly stand upon high moral and religious ground. Fourierism was superhuman in its intention,—in this country, at least. Free-thinking hopes to deliver the soul from the bondage of superstition in all religion. Mormonism was founded as "the Church of Jesus Christ of Latter-Day Saints." Communism at Oneida was professedly built upon the doctrine of human perfection in Christian love. The disaster to the soul is in proportion to the amount of perversion of a living faith. Every movement must be judged, not by what its advocates suppose themselves to believe, but by that which time proves they do believe.

But to return to the Suffrage charge. " American men may quiet their consciences with the delusion that no such injustice exists in this country as in Eastern nations. Though, with the general improvement in our institutions, woman's condition must inevitably have improved also, yet the same principle that degrades her in Turkey insults her here." American men *may* quiet their consciences, while striving to enlighten them further. The answer to Mohammedanism is Turkey. The answer to Christianity is America. Ceremonial uncleanness is absolutely unlike religious and social orderliness in the distribution of duties. How came there to be "general improvement in our institutions?" There has been no improvement in Turkey, in China, in India, or in Japan, except such as is creeping back from the Christendom of which these Suffragists speak with a sneer. Freedom and education have not been appreciably advanced by " woman's becoming a component part of the government " in any land. The lands where she has the most apparent governmental control are the ones that are least educated and least free among those of modern civilization.

The church is an ever-growing body, and its clergy hold widely differing beliefs. The Egyptian priesthood guarded the sacred mysteries and ruled the state. Through the utmost that natural religion can do for man, they had gleaned the secret of a Supreme Maker and Ruler of the universe. Moses, who was " learned in all their wisdom," led the first exiles across the sea to find " freedom to worship God," and, from that day to this, the ministers of religion have stood as public guard over the mysteries of faith and, in the beginnings of each civilization, have ruled the state. Whenever they have forgotten the lesson that Moses taught, the lesson that Paul more clearly taught, that to God alone is any soul responsible, they have proved stumbling-blocks to progress. It is true that religious bigots, as Suffrage writers say, have " defended capital punishment, intemperance, slavery, polygamy, and the subjection of woman." But capital punishment is defended by many besides bigots. Intemperance finds not only its strongest but its most effective

17

foes in the Christian ministry and the Christian church. Slavery in our country rent in twain several great religious bodies. James G. Birney says that " probably nine-tenths of the Abolitionists were church-members." With polygamy came woman's subjection and woman suffrage into our free States. And the bigots outside the Christian ministry and church must share the same condemnation with any who, professing freedom, have yet forgotten the injunction of the Bible and the Christ.

" She would invade the pulpit." Invasion seems a strange word to use in regard to woman's entrance upon one of the highest of human duties. A pulpitless teacher she is and always has been. Missionary women have taught multitudes of beings. The Salvation lassie has no thought of invasion, or of self-exaltation, when she leads the service of a thousand souls ; and I am not willing to believe that a single woman who has entered the regular ministry has any more. It is the spirit of Suffrage that looks upon woman's advance as an attack.

But times have changed, say Suffrage leaders. Mrs. Cornelia K. Hood, in her report of the King's County Suffrage work for 1895, says: " A circular letter was addressed to all the clergymen known to be friends, asking them that a sermon might be preached by them in favor of woman suffrage. This request met with a liberal response, and many able addresses were made on

the Sunday morning set for that purpose." In
her report of the Suffrage campaign in New York
city in the winter of 1895-96, Dr. Jacobi says,
speaking of the parlor meetings : "Several prominent clergymen joined us—Mr. Rainsford, the
Rev. Arthur Brooks, Mr. Percy Grant, Mr. Eaton,
Mr. Leighton Williams." In referring to the last
regular meeting of the County Suffrage Association held that winter in Cooper Union, she says :
" The meeting was addressed by Samuel Gompers,
President of the Federation of Labor, by Dr.
Peters, an Episcopal clergyman, by Father Ducey,
the Catholic priest, Dr. Saunders, a Baptist
minister, and Henry George, the advocate of
single tax." In her address before the Constitutional Convention, she said : " The Church,
which fifty years ago was a unit in denouncing
the public work of woman—even for the slave—
is now divided in its councils." The church
never was a unit in denouncing the public work
of woman, and much of her noblest public work
has been done under its auspices. The behavior
of Suffrage women in slavery times caused
scandal to church and state. The right of private
judgment, claimed always by Protestant Christianity, has divided the clergy on all questions ;
and " a clergyman, a priest, and a minister " were
as free to believe, and to speak what they believed,
on suffrage, as were Samuel Gompers, who lately
offended the Labor organization by inviting two
anarchists to address it, and Henry George, whose

single-tax theories have lately turned law and order upside down in Delaware.

"Interpret the Bible anew from her own standpoint." The volume in which a beginning has been made in this work is a thick pamphlet bearing a motto from Cousin on one cover, and the picture of a piano as an advertisement on the other. It is with a profound sense of sadness and disgust that any woman who honors God and loves her own sex turns its pages. Behold the first dilemma in which the commentators find themselves involved. Mrs. Stanton opens the comments on the Creation as follows: "In the great work of the creation, the crowning glory was realized when man and woman were evolved on the sixth day, the masculine and feminine forces in the image of God, that must have existed eternally, in all forms of matter and mind. . . . How then is it possible to make woman an afterthought? . . . All those theories based on the assumption that man was prior in the creation, have no foundation in Scripture. As to woman's subjection, on which both the canon and civil law delight to dwell, it is important to note that equal dominion is given to woman over every living thing, but not a word is said giving man dominion over woman. No lesson of woman's subjection can be fairly drawn from the first chapter of the Old Testament."

In commenting on the second account of the Creation, Ellen Battelle Dietrick says: "It is

now generally conceded that some one (nobody
pretends to know who) at some time (nobody
pretends to know exactly when) copied two
creation myths on the same leather roll, one immediately following the other. Modern theolo-
gians have, for convenience sake, entitled these
two fables, respectively, the Elohistic and the
Jahoistic stories. They differ not only in the
point I have mentioned above, but in the order of
the 'creative acts,' in regard to the mutual attitude of man and woman, and in regard to human
freedom from prohibitions imposed by deity.
Now, it is manifest that both of these stories
cannot be true; intelligent women who feel
bound to give the preference to either, may
decide according to their own judgment which is
more worthy of an intelligent woman's acceptance. My own opinion is, that the second story
was manipulated by some wily Jew, in an endeavor to give 'heavenly authority' for requiring
a woman to obey the man she married." Lillie
Devereux Blake takes still another horn of the
dilemma. She says: "In the detailed description of creation we find a gradually ascending
series. 'Creeping things,' 'great sea-monsters,'
every bird of wing,' 'cattle and living things of
the earth,' the 'fish of the sea and the birds of
the heavens;' then man, and, last and crowning
glory of the whole, woman. It cannot be maintained that woman was inferior to man, even if,
as asserted in chapter ii., she was created after

him, without at once admitting that man is inferior to the creeping things because created after them."

These commentators, on the whole, agree that the first account of creation does not teach woman's subjection to man; that, although "some wily Jew" inserted the second account in an endeavor to give "heavenly authority for requiring a woman to obey the man she married," he has been outwitted after all, for the ascending series of creation really teaches the same lesson as the first account, and from it woman's inferiority cannot be maintained. And yet it would seem that she must be an "afterthought" if she is to be superior.

Mrs. Stanton, in summing up the concensus of opinion on a matter which is not of the slightest importance to any of them, except that they feel an interest, for the cause of Suffrage, in endeavoring to release woman from the long bondage of superstition, says: "The first account dignifies woman as an important factor in the creation, equal in power and glory with man. The second makes her a mere afterthought. The world in good running order without her, the only reason for her advent being the solitude of man. There is something sublime in bringing order out of chaos; light out of darkness; giving each planet its place in the solar system; oceans and lands their limits,—wholly inconsistent with a petty surgical operation to find material for the mother of the race. It is in this allegory that all the enemies of woman rest their battering-rams, to prove her inferiority. Accepting the view that man was prior in the creation, some Scriptural writers say that, as the woman was of the man, therefore her position should be one of subjection. Grant it. Then, as the historical fact is reversed in our day, and the man is now of the woman, shall his place be one of subjection? The equal position declared in the first account must prove more satisfactory to both sexes; created alike in the image of God—the heavenly Mother and Father. Thus, the Old Testament, 'in the beginning,' proclaims the simultaneous creation of man and woman, the eternity and equality of sex; and the New Testament echoes back through the centuries the individual sovereignty of woman growing out of this natural fact. Paul, in speaking of equality as the very soul and essence of Christianity, said, 'There is neither Jew nor Greek, there is neither bond nor free, there is neither male nor female; for ye are all one in Christ Jesus. With this recognition of the feminine element in the Godhead in the Old Testament, and this declaration of the equality of the sexes in the New, we may well wonder at the contemptible status woman occupies in the Christian Church to-day."

So the woman who spurns the Bible as the book that is responsible for woman's degradation, who denies that it is the word of God, who pours

out upon Paul the vials of her wrath, finds in
them both her highest warrant for believing in
the "equal position" of woman, "the perfect
equality of the sexes." When the wrath of woman
thus praises God, the one who believes that
through woman's status in the Bible and in the
Christian Church this perfect equality is being
worked out day by day need not take up con-
troversial cudgels. Ribaldry in woman seems
more gross than in man, and this is woman's
ribaldry. It is profane to speak of the "feminine
element in the Godhead." God is a spirit. There
is no more a feminine than a masculine element
in the Godhead. Sex belongs to mortal life and
its conditions. It begins and ends with this earth.
Christ has told us so : There will be in another
world "no marrying, nor giving in marriage, but
we all shall be as the angels in heaven." The
equality of which Paul spoke as "the very soul
and essence of Christianity " is the equality of the
essence and soul of male and female humanity,
and the oneness of the believer's soul with that
of the Christ in whom his soul believes. The
soul of humanity, as well as its body, is bound
by sex conditions as long as it draws the breath
of this transitory life. Every thought and every
act reveal the governing power of the sex mould
in which its form is cast for this world's uses.
The use of this world is to give preparation for
another and a better one; final spiritual triumph
is the end to be attained. Humanity is now in

the image of God only in the essential sense in
which the full corn in the ear may be said to be
wrapped up in its kernel, and it can unfold only
according to the laws of its being. The first account of Creation sets forth, with the beautiful
imagery of the Orient, the general and ultimate
truth. The second account, with the same grand
simplicity, foreshadows the method and the long,
slow process by which this ultimate end is to be
attained.

In continuing their comments, the editors say :
" In chapter v., verse 23, Adam proclaims the
eternal oneness of the happy pair, ' This is now
bone of my bone and flesh of my flesh ;' no hint
of her subordination. How could men, admitting
these words to be divine revelation, ever have
preached the subjection of woman ? Next comes
the naming of the mother of the race. ' She shall
be called woman,' in the ancient form of the
word, ' womb-man.' She was man and more than
man, because of her maternity. The assertion of
the supremacy of the woman in the marriage relation is contained in chapter v., 24 : ' Therefore
shall a man leave his father and his mother and
cleave unto his wife.' Nothing is said of the
headship of man, but he is commanded to make her
the head of the household, the home, a rule followed for centuries under the Matriarchate."

A rule that has been followed rudely through
all centuries, and is followed to-day with far
greater approach to perfect obedience. Mater-

nity was to be God's method of working out
the problem of changing the innocence of ignorant savagery to the holiness of enlightened civilization.    To this end, the more delicate and complex organism of the womb-man must be cared
for by the strength and steadiness that could find
full play because that subtler task was not demanded of it.

In commenting on chapter iii., which contains
the account of the Garden of Eden and the eating
of the apple, they say: " As out of this allegory
grow the doctrines of original sin, the fall of man
and of woman the author of all our woes, and the
curses on the serpent, the woman and the man,
the Darwinian theory of the gradual growth of
the race from a lower to a higher  type of animal
life is more hopeful and encouraging."

The Christian doctrine is more hopeful and encouraging still.   It reveals the growth of the race
from a low type of animal life to  the perfect life
of the soul.

We do not need to go back to the garden where
our first parents dwelt, to look for the substan-
tiation of the eternal truth of this whole wondrous
story.   Amid the landscape of the civilization of
the noblest country that the world  possesses, we
have the drama repeated.   In the work of Anne
Hutchinson, Ann Lee, Frances Wright, Lucretia
Mott, Elizabeth Stanton, Susan Anthony, Ellen
Dietrick, Lillie Blake, and their fellow-commen-
tators, we have re-enacted the Temptress and the

Fall. Woman first aspired. She stretched forth her eager hand to seize the good, and in so doing snatched the evil that grew beside it. The woman in Eden had not learned what maternity taught her later—that she could point the path, but could not lead in entering it. Wherever woman has forgotten this hard-won but glorious lesson, she has been the most dangerous of guides. The conscience, that intellect of the soul, woke first in woman. By her obedience to its voice, the faith that worketh by love had its perfected work, and the promise that was given to her was fulfilled in the birth of Christ. A Creation story without a gospel is chaos without gravitation, primal darkness without the sun. Forward to divinity in human form woman was able, through obedience, to point mankind. Backward to divinity in human form she points again, until humanity itself shall become divine. If she loses the final vision, or substitutes her own, she can neither point nor guide. No wonder woman has been a mystery to the church. No wonder a witch was not allowed to live, while a wizard might; she was more dangerous. No wonder Paul was perplexed by the woman question. No wonder monks fled to the desert. Christ has spoken the final words of woman, "Thy faith hath saved thee." From the anguish of His cross he said: "Woman, behold thy son!" "Behold thy mother," and the beloved disciple "took her to his own home from that hour."

In the Suffrage appeal of 1860, the writers said : "The difference between husband and wife is as vast as the difference between Christ and his Church." Christ himself says that the difference between him and his Church is that of degree, not of kind, and that the resemblance is that of essential oneness. He says: "I am the vine, ye are the branches." Could union be more completely pictured? The fruit-bearing branch cannot say to the strength-giving vine, " I have no need of thee." The vine cannot say, " I have no need of thee." Man in his imperious folly has pictured the relationship as that of oak and vine which have no organic union; but, despite imperiousness and folly, both men and women, through mutual obedience to God, have thus far worked out, and are still working out, the nobler destiny for both.

In summing up their opinion of the Pentateuch, the editors of the Suffrage Woman's Bible say : " This utter contempt for all the decencies of life, and all the natural personal rights of women, as set forth in these pages, should destroy, in the minds of women at least, all authority to superhuman origin, and stamp the Pentateuch at least as emanating from the most obscene minds of a barbarous age." So low can woman fall in ignorance and shameless audacity when the faith that works by love is lost. As the spirit of the Commandments comes to prevail, the decencies of life and the natural personal rights of woman become more secure. Here again Christ has spoken the

ultimate word. He says: "Ye have heard by
them of old time 'Thou shalt not commit adultery,'
but I say unto you whosoever looketh on a woman
to lust after her hath committed adultery with
her already in his heart." This is the standard of
chastity to which mankind must come. When
the Hebrew mother in living faith cast the bread
of her own life's being upon the Nile, she was to
find it after many days in the great law-giver of
her people. The Commandments received through
him were the foreshadowing of those greater
oracles in which Christ summed up the whole
duty of man. The individual liberty which
Moses was the first to proclaim to a whole people,
in the Pentateuch, Christ, his anti-type, proclaimed
to a whole world, and on his proclamation rests
to-day the freedom of woman and of the American Republic. The Bread of Life, again cast on
the troubled waters of this world, by woman's
faith, through Mary the Virgin Mother, is return-
ing after many days.

Strange that we should forever turn back, as if
the application of any essential truth were finished.
The child walks by faith. The childhood of the
world walked by faith, and left in the Bible the
evidence of things that are not seen but are eternal. The Suffrage movement has a quarrel with
the Bible because the Creator is there represented,
for the reverence of the race, under the guise of a
Heavenly Father, and not a Heavenly Mother, or
rather, not as a human pair, equal in dignity and

power.  If the first impulsion of love toward God
had come into this world through the mind of
man, he would have represented the divine love
that his soul conceived under the guise of that
being on earth whom he most loved.  But love
was born with the "disabilities" of woman ; it
was evolved through motherhood ; and the same
impulse that gave it, exalted, not itself, but what
it loved and trusted.  " I have gotten a man from
the Lord" said the first recorded mother, who
had learned to know the Lord through motherhood ; and the boy she bore was taught to look
up with confidence to the strength and protection
of his father.  She told him that the pity of his
father, which made him bring food and raiment,
and which guarded his home, was an image of the
feeling that was felt for him by the divine being.
Could man have learned the lesson first, we can
see that the story would have been different, because man has named every beautiful and gracious
thing for woman.  Virtue, temperance, truth,
purity, love, faith, hope, liberty, grace, beauty,
charity, the inspirers of art and science, of music
and literature, of justice and of religion, all are
feminine.  When man says: " Our Father which
art in heaven," he prays as his mother taught him.
Through the self-abnegation that was unconscious
of its sacrifice, woman was to be the instrument
for bringing human life up, on, to the God who,
being spirit, could act upon a clay-bound mind
only through the highest human thing that love

could know. Men, as well as women, have mis-
understood and misinterpreted this. The love
that "is not puffed up," "doth not behave itself
unseemly," cannot proclaim its own virtue—to ar-
rogate it is to lose it. But the secret of the Lord
has been with those who feared Him, and it has
led the world aright in spite of blunder and of sin.

If man, in his ignorant conceit, has fancied that
this was the subjection of woman, it has been a
part of his mother's lesson to correct that impression. If woman, in her folly, has allowed herself
to make the same mistake, that, too, is working
out its cure through the love that so arranged
human nature that "a man should leave father
and mother and cleave unto his wife, and they
twain should be one flesh," and that "*her desire*
should be to her husband*" in those matters wherein the mutual interest required that he should
bear sway. If there is a minister of religion who
holds to the perverted notion that, because woman
ate the original apple in disobedience to God's
command, she was the bringer of original sin into
the world, and for that was and is punished by
arbitrary subjection to the authority of man, that
minister does not deserve the support of women.
The fact that he would have few listeners, and
fewer followers, if women were not the bringers
and the maintainers of religious faith is sufficient
proof against such an exposition of scripture. As
a matter of fact, while the dogmatism of belief,
like the dogmatism of unbelief, has made asser-

tions that have dishonored both divine and human nature, the practical working of formulated faiths of all names has been to approach the standard laid down in the Old and the New Testament. The model of being set by Christ is that of a little child. "Except ye become as little children, ye shall in no wise enter the kingdom of heaven." The natural characteristics of the child are faith, and hope, and love—the virtues that abide. When the virile apostle to the Gentiles " put away childish things," he kept these childlike qualities. If woman first attains them in perfection, she is superior; if man, he is superior. In the race toward the final goal, to be equal in accomplishment it is needful to be equal in obedience. The keynote of Paul's preaching was obedience—the obedience of all human beings to God in Christ, the obedience of all men and women to lawful civil authority for the sake of Christ and the promotion of his kingdom,—the obedience of men to one another in the churchly offices, for the sake of that " decency " that he loved and enjoined—the obedience of the equal wife to the husband who was the external representative of family life.

With Eastern nations the veil was the sign of retirement, of domestic life, and it was assumed by wives when they were in the street or in a public assembly. In heathen and barbarous countries it was also deemed a sign of woman's subjection and inferiority. The Hebrews were the first people to attain any truly spiritual conceptions, and they began to have a commensurately higher idea of the possibilities of woman's nature and work. When Christian women, in their new-found freedom, would have thrown aside the veil, just as Christian men, in their new-found reverence for God, would have repudiated the heathen wife, Paul said to them both that Christian liberty was individual,—it changed the character, not the sex relations. In arranging for church discipline, he advised that men should uncover the head, and women should wear the veil. But he said, in reference to that veil, that "woman should have *power* on her head, because of the angels." The angels are spoken of in the New Testament as veiling their faces in the very presence of the Creator. In that truer symbolism of Christianity, man was to uncover his head in token of reverence to God and acceptance of the responsibility of the guardianship of the earth. Woman was to cover her head in token of her acceptance of man's guardianship and of her dominion over his heart, to which she had revealed God's will.

Paul adds: "For as the woman is of the man, so is the man also of the woman; but all things are of God." This relation was one of the mysteries that Paul said he did not comprehend, nor could he, till the lessons he taught should work out their results, and might serve as commentary.

Life itself, as well as all that life could come to mean, depended upon woman's consenting. The

18

word "obey" in some marriage services seems, like what it really is, a survival. Obedience has brought its reward, and the consent of the heart is more than the consent of the lips. But if there is no consent of the heart to wifehood and mother-hood, in time there will be no chivalry, no prog-ress, no final emancipation for the race. Con-senting is also commanding, and woman loses her life in order to find it in the fulfillment of her wish. It was consent to her own teaching. The chivalrous and tender-hearted Paul, who spoke of women with reverent affection, who adopted as his own the mother of Rufus, was re-peating the lesson of every Jewish mother from Sarah to Deborah, and from Deborah to the women who were last at Christ's cross and first beside his tomb. Deborah, who was the judge, prophetess and poet, but first of all "a mother in Israel," under whom her degenerate people had peace for forty years, rebuked Barak and said, to their humiliation: "This day shall the Lord de-liver Israel by the hand of a woman." From this teaching Paul uttered his rebuke to the wayward church at Corinth: "It is a shame for a man to cover his head, inasmuch as he is the image and glory of God; but the woman is the glory of the man." And he added, in speaking of the wear-ing of the veil, "For this cause ought the woman to have power" "because of the angels." In the Epistle to the Ephesians Paul admonishes the Church to be "imitators of God, as beloved children, and walk in love, even as Christ also loved you, and gave himself for you, an offering and a sacrifice to God for a sweet-smelling savour." Again, he says: "Therefore, as the Church is subject unto Christ, so let the wives be to their own husbands in everything." And as if to make doubly certain that no one should think that such submission implied bondage or inequality, he adds "Husbands, love your wives even as Christ also loved the Church *and gave himself for it.*" Again, he says: "So ought men to love their wives, as their own bodies. . . . Even as the Lord the Church," adding with almost strained Oriental vehemence, "for we are members of his body, of his flesh and of his bones. For this cause shall a man leave his father and his mother, and shall be joined unto his wife, and they twain shall be one flesh."

The comment most readily suggested is, that through this teaching the use of the veil has now no such significance. The uncovering of the head is a token of respect, largely to woman. The retention of the bonnet is not dreamed of in connection with woman's relation to man, nor does it suggest woman's power in the moral world. The obedience through which love "constrained" a mind that had been bred to forms, was free If anybody now holds that woman was intended to glorify God indirectly, through man, or to serve God by serving man, he makes an assumption long discredited, and not in accord with the spirit of Christ and of Paul. Man is as much the glory of woman as woman is the glory of man, and they reveal equally the glory of God.

In speaking of the proprieties of life, Paul said: "Does not nature herself teach you?" "If a man have long hair, it is a shame to him." "If a woman have long hair, it is a glory to her." The badge of womanhood is a glory, and the "short-haired women and long-haired men" of the early Suffrage movement transformed the symbols of dignity and honor into those of contempt and disgrace.

Canon law grew up during the Middle Ages, when came the great

> "Death-grapple in the darkness, 'twixt old systems and the Word."

The wondrous church that rose on the ruins of Roman militarism, and overthrew Norman feudalism, gave evidence, in its code, of the bitterness of the conflict and the rudeness of the time. The legal fiction that, in acknowledging the oneness of husband and wife, yet made the husband that one, was a perversion of Scripture.

It has been publicly said by Suffragists from the first, that the tenets of the Church of Rome, in which Canon law had its origin, were inimical to woman suffrage; and they have further said that those who canonize women and worship the Virgin Mother, should naturally have been friendly to the Suffrage idea. I suppose no one will deny that the spirit of the Roman body is that of a state church. I have no more to say in criticism of it as a Christian denomination than I have of others; but that organization which has held temporal and spiritual power to be co-ordinate and interdependent in government, presents a political phase that has direct bearing on my theme, and I make my few comments as a historian. The Church that inculcates Mariolatry would have far more ignorant women to add to our body of voters than any other. It has done less for woman's education and general advancement than any other, but its claims are not therefore modest. The school elections in Staten Island last year gave an object-lesson in regard to its intention to use the suffrage. In Connecticut, the school election presented another evidence of the intense interest felt by the Catholic clergy in public-school matters. In California, in the late canvass for woman suffrage, that Church assisted largely in carrying on the work to secure the amendment. While many of its individual members are among the noblest friends that civil and religious freedom have in our country, this church, by its traditions, and by its latest pronunciamentos, shows itself as a force that, for its own selfish reasons, may be reckoned on the side of woman suffrage in its conflict with woman's progress.

# CHAPTER X.

THE ninth count of the Suffrage Declaration says : "He has created a false sentiment by giving to the world a different code of morals for men and women, by which moral delinquencies which exclude woman from society, are not only tolerated, but deemed of little account in men." And the list of grievances is summed up as follows : "Because women do feel themselves aggrieved, oppressed and fraudulently deprived of their most sacred rights, we insist that they have immediate admission to all the rights and privileges which belong to them as citizens of the United States."

The writers do not say whether the code of morals referred to is a code of law or an unwritten code of public sentiment. If they mean the former, their statement is not true; for whatever laws affect moral delinquencies visit their penalties equally upon men and women. If they mean public sentiment alone, the answer is, that both men and women are responsible for its creation. It is folly to deny that there is, in

278

the nature of things, more excuse for men than for women. A mother realizes that her son has a natural temptation of which her daughter knows nothing. But this fact, while it accounts in part for the different standard, by no means exonerates man. One of the strangest anomalies of human experience exists in connection with this matter. Man reposes his deepest faith in the existence of goodness at its vital point, in the virtue of woman; and yet when he tramples upon that virtue he screens himself behind the excuse that her nature is as vulnerable as his own, while his temptation is greater. The main reason, as it seems to me, why women often appear more cruel to their fallen sisters than do men, lies in the fact that pure women abhor this vice as they abhor no other. Besides bestowing upon woman a loftier moral sense, her Creator has hedged about her virtue with a feeling of physical repulsion that is distinct from the moral question involved. The social life of the world is to a large extent in woman's hands. When she says to men "You cannot bring your impurity into my home," "You must be the ones to guard our sons and daughters," the reform will be begun in earnest. Woman's faith, and her abstract way of looking at moral questions, prevent her from fastening her thought, as men naturally do, on any special culprit, in her severe but vague sense of wrong in this matter. The Suffragists have taken fewer steps in the direction of removing the social

plague-spot than in the direction of bringing
about a system of easier divorce—a thing that
strikes a blow directly against, instead of for, the
virtue of their sex.   Social opinion is causing a
change in some of the laws concerning social vice.
Nearly every State legislature has raised the
age of consent.   So far as Suffrage associations
have assisted in this, it proves their ability and
their good will; but much more is due to our educated physicians and philanthropists.

It seems at first thought as if there were no
direct connection between voting and social questions of sex; but I am following the lead of my
Suffrage texts.   Others who attempt the discussion are led to the same themes.   Dr. Jacobi, in
her book, says : " The problem is, to show why,
in a representative system based on the double
principle that all the intelligence in the state shall
be enlisted for its welfare, and all the weakness in the state represented for its own defence,
women, being often intelligent, and often weak,
and always persons in the community, should not
also be represented."   In replying to the anti-
suffrage arguments of Prof. Goldwin Smith, she
says:   " Do sex relations depend upon acts of
Parliament or constitutional amendments?   Can
women marry a ballot, or embrace the franchise,
otherwise than by a questionable figure of speech?
Must adultery and infanticide necessarily be
favored by the decisions of female jurors?   Is
divorce legislation, as arranged by the exclusive

wisdom of men, now so satisfactory that women
—who must perforce be involved in every case—
should always modestly refrain from attempting
amendment? This entire class of considerations,
however irrelevant to the issue, may be grouped
together and considered together, because, to a
large class of minds—the rudest, quite as much as
those of Mr. Smith's cultivation—they are the
considerations that do come to the front whenever equal rights are suggested." She adds that
the reason they come to the front is, "that men,
accustomed to think of men as possessing sex
attributes and other things besides, are accustomed to think of women as having sex and nothing else."

Is there a ruder mind anywhere than one that
could not only think but write a sentiment so
revolting and so false? And yet the statement
admits that, whatever the reason, the sex issue
does underlie the whole Suffrage question.

In their "History," the leaders not only set
forth all the specific charges in their Declaration
of Sentiments, but of this "rebellion such as the
world has never seen" they say: "Men saw that
with political equality for woman, she could no
longer be kept in social subjection. The fear of a
social revolution thus complicated the discussion."

In the Introduction to the Suffrage Woman's
Bible, the commentators say: "How can woman's
position be changed from that of a subordinate
to an equal, without opposition?—without the

broadest discussion of all the questions involved in her present degradation? For so far-reaching and momentous a reform as her complete independence, an entire revolution in all existing institutions is inevitable."

Dr. Jacobi says: "To-day, when all men rule, and diffused self-government has abolished the old divisions between the governing classes and the governed, only one class remains over whom all men can exercise sovereignty—namely, the women. Hence a shuddering dread runs through society at the proposal to also abolish this last refuge of facile domination."

Here, then, all these Suffragists present a problem far more momentous than appears when it is proposed "to show why, in a representative system based on the double principle that all the intelligence in the state shall be enlisted for its welfare, and all the weakness in the state represented for its defence, women, being often intelligent, and often weak, and always persons, should not also be represented." It is the sex battle that has been waged from the beginning. In the Suffrage Woman's Bible Mrs. Stanton says: "The correction of this [the misinterpretation of the Bible as concerns woman] will restore her, and deprive her enemy, man, of a reason for his oppression and a weapon of attack." Disguise it as they may, to themselves and to others, the Suffrage idea is compelled to claim that man is woman's enemy, that the ballot is the engine of his power, and that therefore she must vote. The reason that "these considerations come to the front whenever equal rights is mentioned" is because the women of that movement brought them there, and keep them there, and because no one can seriously consider the matter without seeing that they belong there.

In discussing them, Dr. Jacobi says : " What is imagined, claimed, and very seriously demanded, is, that women be recognized as human beings, with a range of faculties and activities co-extensive with that of men, whatever may be the difference in the powers within that range."

In another place she admits that " women are really recognized as individuals, the same as men," and the fact that they are so recognized is made the basis of an argument for their voting. Suppose men demanded that they be given a " range of faculties and activities co-extensive with that of women, whatever may be the difference in the powers within that range," if they demanded it " seriously " they would probably become laughing-stocks.

She says : " The sex relations of women as lovers, as wives, as mothers, as daughters, remain untouched, certainly unimpaired, by the demand to extend beyond these. What is impaired is not the sex relation, nor sex condition, but the social disabilities, the personal and social subordination, the condition of political non-existence, which have been foisted upon that sex condition."

The repeated demand to " extend beyond " the sex relations of either sex *is* a demand to touch those relations, and whether it is a demand to impair them depends upon the question whether it is true that disabilities and subordination have been foisted upon the sex conditions. In olden times they were. Men were subject to social disabilities, personal and social subordination, and political non-existence. It followed that women were also in the same subjection. As men threw off the yoke, the sex relations began to assume their natural position. Man was the protector, woman the protected. In the natural relations, the protector is at the service of the protected, and that is the state of things to-day. In order to be preserved in bodily, mental, and spiritual freedom, woman must yield with grace to the hand that serves her. In order to protect, man must see to it that this freedom he has won is kept sacred and inviolable. He cannot be at once a tyrant and a guard. This freedom removes from woman all disabilities save those of sex. The question then is, can all the intelligence and all the weakness of women be represented for their own welfare and their own defence, by the same methods as those by which men attain that end, and yet leave these fundamental sex relations untouched and unimpaired ?

The Suffrage leaders did not expect or intend to leave them untouched, or unimpaired, if complete change was impairment. In the " History " they say: "It is often asked if political equality would not arouse antagonism between the sexes? If it could be proved that men and women had been harmonious in all ages and countries, and that women were happy and satisfied in their slavery, we might hesitate in proposing any change whatever; but the apathy, the helpless, hopeless resignation of a subject class, cannot be called happiness. A woman growing up under American ideas of liberty in government and religion cannot brook any disability based on sex alone, without a deep feeling of antagonism with the power that creates it."

Dr. Jacobi says: "Manhood Suffrage in America may seem to result, historically, from the general average equality of social conditions among the inhabitants of the Thirteen States. But it may also be deduced as a philosophical necessity from the Idea of Individualism, which became the core of the Federal Union. This idea, at first suggested only for men, has, little by little, spread to women also."

Individualism, in the sense of personal moral responsibility, became the core, first of the Hebrew Theocracy, and last of the American National life. But that republicanism which has come to rest on sex distinction is the combined result of Individualism and Authority. Suffrage discussion for years has turned upon the idea of Individualism *versus* Authority.

In a government like ours, where all the intelligence and all the weakness *are* represented for their own welfare and defence, authority must to a certain extent hold a stern hand over individualism, because freedom for all means license for not a single one, be it man or woman. Mrs. Fanny Ames says: " Any argument [against Suffrage] worth anything at all, comes down to this—an argument against American democracy—and must rest there." Many arguments have been adduced against Woman Suffrage that were also arguments against democracy ; because there are always people, and wise people too, who fear the test of the ultimate experiment. To this fear the Suffragists catered when, in contradiction to their own dictum of universal suffrage, they asked Congress for a sixteenth amendment that should require an educational qualification for all, both men and women. But, guided by the statesmanship that seeks to form a true and enduring democracy, this Republic has come to the sex basis.

Dr. Jacobi says: " The complex contradictions in the present distributions of sovereign power are further intensified by the vulgarization of the general ideal. It is one thing to say, 'Some men shall rule,' quite another to declare, 'All men shall rule,' and that in virtue of the most primitive and rudimentary attribute they possess,—that, namely, of sex. If the original contempt for masses of men has ever diminished, and the conception of mankind been ennobled, it is because, upon the primitive animal foundation, human

imagination has built a fair structure of mental
and moral attribute and possibility, and habitually
deals with that. This indeed is no new thing
to do; for it was to this moral man that Pericles
addressed his funeral oration, and of whom Lincoln thought in his speech at Gettysburg. Of
this moral man, women—the sex hitherto so
despised—are now recognized to constitute an
integral part. It is useless, therefore, to attempt
to throw them out by an appeal to the primitive
conditions of a physical force to which no one
appeals for any other purpose."

The immortal orator at Gettysburg was com-
mander-in-chief of an army and navy whose physical power was then in the very act of saving the
nation and redeeming it from the sin of slavery.
The soldier-statesman of Greece, in his funeral oration, was addressing an army. The fair structure
of mental and moral attribute and possibility has
not been built by human imagination. The conception of the moral man that has ennobled mankind is older than any man who has embodied it.
It is as old as mankind itself, upon whose primitive animal foundation God implanted side by
side the conception of the moral man, woman—
and of the governing man, man.

That no inequality should be possible when
this idea should really rest upon the most primitive, rudimentary and yet continuing and controlling attribute, instead of upon complex contradictions in regard to the distribution of sovereign

human power, God, speaking through the ideal
which the moral man had grasped, said: " Therefore shall a man leave his father and his mother,
and shall cleave unto his wife, and they twain
shall be one flesh."

Man is not the hereditary sovereign in a republic.
He is an actual, present, continuing sovereign, and
he is that only so long as he obeys the law of his
being and constitutes himself, by reason of his
manhood strength, the defence of the republic's
laws for all. In woman suffrage democracy has
met a most dangerous foe. It has been asked
" If it would be best for man to make over half
his sovereignty to woman?" I cannot imagine
how he could do this, whatever might be his wish.
Sovereignty in a republic is only divisible among
those who are equals as to sovereign power; and
any effort to divide with those who lack the essential attribute must result in despotism or anarchy. Men are as subject to the restrictions and
requirements of sex as are women, and when they
try an experiment contrary to those conditions,
the end must be destruction of government itself.

Prof. Goldwin Smith says: "One of the feat-
ures of a revolutionary era is the prevalence of a
feeble facility of abdication. The holders of power,
however natural and legitimate it may be, are too
ready to resign it on the first demand. . . . The
nerves of authority are shaken by the failure of
conviction."

This is true, and it is what makes the present

situation portentous. From the very tender-heartedness of the men of our time comes the danger to the women of this nation. So far from desiring to hold the slightest restriction over the women of the Republic, they may rush into an attempt at abdication of a sovereignty that did not originate in their will but in their environment, in order to prove the sincerity of their desire that woman should not even appear to be compelled to obey.

This movement is a feature of the revolutionary era that seems suddenly to have extended to the men with whose theories it belongs. Not at once, nor everywhere equally, but finally and completely would this change come. Man, as well as woman, must " consent to be governed " by the laws of being. If man really could " share his sovereignty," there might be some show of reason in the Suffrage claim that he should do so. But unless he can abdicate the very essentials of his sex condition, he cannot abdicate his sovereignty. His laws are dead letters whenever more men than those who passed them and approve them choose that they shall be dead. He would have no material outside the men in this country, with which to execute the wishes of the woman voters whom it is proposed to introduce to make laws which they know they cannot themselves enforce.

And this leads us right round again to consider the " disabilities foisted upon sex conditions." The first thing demanded of a voter is that, in the

19

ordinary state of things, he should be able to vote. A body of citizens is asking that a sex be admitted to franchise when it is known to all that a large part of that sex would at every election find it physically impossible, or improper, to go to the polls. Suffragists say: "No women need vote who do not wish to; but they have no right to hinder us." Is this the Individualism of Democracy? It is the Individualism of Anarchy. It is not the rule of the majority. It is class rule with a vengeance; and as for "consenting to be governed," there never was a man or a government that so coolly assumed to govern without their consent such a body, as do the Suffragists. The disabilities "foisted upon sex" would be felt first of all by the wives and mothers who are most interested in the laws.

The next duty of citizenship is jury service. The leaders said: "We demand, in criminal cases, that most sacred of all rights, trial by jury of our own peers." In regard to jury duty Suffragists are not agreed; which fact alone shows that that service would be felt to be an impairment of sex conditions. So impossible has jury duty been found, even in small communities, that in Wyoming the jury service of women ceased with the first judge who admitted them to serve at all; and in Colorado but one or two women have ever served. The judges there do not allow them to be called. It was found to be expensive, and not promotive of the ends of justice. Whether this is held to be man's cruel withholding of woman's rights or not, it shows that either the sex condition or the co-extensiveness of woman's work with man's must be impaired. Dr. Jacobi says in regard to jury service: " The numerous cases for exemption now admitted for men would be certainly paralleled for women, but they would not always be identical. Men are now more often excused for business; women would be excused on the plea of ill-health. Of course the special plea of family cares with young children would rule out thousands of women during a number of years of their lives."

Who would establish the "special plea" for so large a proportion of the voting population? No law of justice on which a solid government can rest could do it; and that it would be asked, and needed, shows that sex conditions would interfere with voting conditions. A criminal case often lasts weeks, even months, during which time the jury are kept together and alone, locked up at night, and walked out by day. This second duty cannot be, and is not, performed; not because many women would not make good jurors, not because they should not try delicate cases, and might not serve well at certain times, and in special ways, but because jury duty, like military service, cannot take account of sex conditions when they are the rule and not the exception.

Office-holding is the next necessary concomitant of the ballot. Of course it can be said at once: "Why, multitudes of men never hold office, why should women?" It may be answered that multitudes of men do hold office, that no American would think of extending the ballot without expecting that, as an accompaniment, the duty, or the privilege, of office-holding should follow.

Not only is it true that if more than half the population were added to the voting list multitudes among them would attempt to rush into office, but it was mainly for office that a majority of those who have been pressing the demand cared for the vote. The authors of the "History" say: "As to offices, it is not be supposed that the class of men now elected will resign to women their chances, and, if they should to any extent, the necessary number of women to fill the offices would make no apparent change in our social circles. If, for example, the Senate of the United States should be entirely composed of women, but two in each State would be withdrawn from the pursuit of domestic happiness."

How could "the class of men now elected" help resigning, if women enough chose to put up ·a woman and give her a majority of votes,—provided, as Suffragists say, that the vote secures the office and retains it by a mere mandate? But it is not one office, or set of offices, which we have to consider. It is the entrance upon political life, permanently, of a large body of women. What that means to the social life that "would not miss them," we well know. There could be no domestic ties; no hindering child. The time would be short before this unnatural position would breed a race of Aspasias—without the intellect that ruled "the ruler of the land, when Athens was the land of fame."

The "History" says: "An honest fear is sometimes expressed 'that women would degrade politics, and politics would degrade women,'" and the writers answer: " As the influence of woman has been uniformly elevating in new civilizations, in missionary work in heathen lands, in schools, colleges, literature, and general society, it is fair to suppose that politics would prove no exception." We do not need to depend upon forecast or inference. The influence of women upon politics, and the influence of politics upon women, have already been degrading. This is true of political intrigue in the old world, and of the " Female Lobby " in Washington. It is astonishing to what an extent it is true in our new country, with our fresh and sweet traditions.

In 1851, Mrs. Stanton, writing to a convention at Akron, Ohio, said: "The great work before us is the education of those just coming on the stage of action. Begin with the girls of to-day, and in twenty years we can revolutionize this nation. Teach the girl to go alone by night and day, if need be, on the lonely highway, or through the busy streets of the crowded metropolis. Better for her to suffer occasional insults, or die outright, than live the life of a coward, or never move without a protector. . . . Teach her that it is no part of life to cater to the prejudices of those around her. Make her independent of public sentiment, by showing her how worthless and rotten a thing it is. . . . Think you, women thus educated would long remain the weak, dependent beings we now find them? They would soon settle for themselves this whole question of Woman's Rights."

Fifty years of such teaching has had its effect. The fine bloom has too often been brushed from our girls' delicacy of thought. They can strut through the street in the daytime wearing a shirt-front, a cravat, a choker, a vest, and a man's hat, and carrying a cane. A few can flaunt themselves in bloomers and knickerbockers, and ride astride a bicycle. They ape men in everything except courtesy to women. But the result is not what was expected. These customs have introduced the chaperone, and have put an end to simple freedom between boys and girls. The Puritan maiden in her modesty could let John Alden speak for himself, because the John who could summon courage to speak of love to such a girl would not dare to breathe impurity. When the young woman requires a social spy, the young man is apt to forget that her innocent dignity is her own best guardian. With the passing of the " lady," American women may fail to remember that a gentlewoman need pretend to no aristocracy but that of the *noblesse oblige* of her own femininity. In the paragraph quoted above, women are spoken of as those who are " uniformly elevating " and as " weak and dependent " to a contemptuous degree. They cannot be both at once, and it seems to me that in fact they are neither. Woman is not an angel nor a demon, not a conqueror nor a slave. But the seed from which any of these conflicting natures may develop lies in more fertile soil, within her impassioned and impressible soil, than in man's. The Suffrage movement will leave her much better or worse than it found her. The phrase " the new woman," with the instinctive explanation that she " is as refined, or as good a wife, mother, sister, daughter, housekeeper," as the old, is ominous.

Suffrage writers seem to hold two views in regard to sex. One is, that it is so pervasive that it cannot be affected by any line of conduct. The other is, that, so far as mind is concerned, it is purely a fanciful barrier, and the less there appears of external distinction the better will this be realized. The Suffrage " History " says : " Sex pervades all matter. Whatever it is, it requires no special watchfulness on our part to see that it is maintained." At the same time the dictum " There is no sex in mind," has been a Suffrage war-cry. It seems to me that both views are unscientific and dangerous to social morals. Sex integrity is pervasive of the whole nature only when men and women are true to the ideal of the essential distinctions in each. The true environment of woman is womanliness; not to fit her nature to the utmost that womanliness can mean to the world, is to fail of womanly attainment. But making herself a distorted woman cannot make her even an imperfect man. The mere act of going to the polls is not unwomanly ; it might be as proper as going to the post-office ; but attempting to encroach upon duty that is laid upon man in her behalf is neither womanly nor manly.

In demanding equality, Suffragists assume that there is not and has not been equality. In asserting that "there is no sex in mind," they really have had to maintain that there is one sex in mind, and that the masculine, to which woman must conform. If man wanted clinching arguments to prove his superiority, could he find another to match this one which suffrage has furnished him ? The quaint wit of the Yankee put it neatly when he gave the toast, "Woman— once our superior, now our equal!" Man has said: "The hand that rocks the cradle rules the world." He has also said, with Martin : "Whatever may be the customs and laws of a country, the women of it decide the morals." The civilization of no nation has risen higher than the carrying out of the religious ideals of its best womanhood. If man has the outward framing of church and state, woman has the framing of the character of man. There is no schism in the body of human duties as the Lord established them. The issues have become more distinctly and openly moral issues; and in so far as woman can make it consist with that inner life of the home and the child, which alone can make the family and fix the state on any sure foundation, she is welcomed by man to meet the common foe. Such new avenues to wealth and distinction as she can enter with womanly dignity and grace will open to her as fast as man can make them places where she can walk with security and comfort to herself and advantage to them both. And they will open no faster.

The woman Suffragist has had to wage as bitter a warfare against physical science as against religion. Eliza Burt Gamble, in her volume which discusses "The Evolution of Woman," takes up the cudgels against both the Bible and man's scientific classification of woman, or rather his failure to classify her properly at all. She says: " When we bear in mind the past experience of the human race, it is not perhaps surprising that, during an era of physical force and the predominance of the animal instincts in man, the doctrine of male superiority should have become firmly grounded. But with the dawn of scientific investigation it might have been hoped that the prejudices resulting from a lower condition of human society would disappear. When, however, we turn to the most advanced scientific writers of the present century, we find that the prejudices which throughout thousands of years have been gathering strength are by no means eradicated. Mr. Darwin, whenever he had occasion to touch on the mental capacities of women, or, more particularly, the relative capacities of the sexes, manifested the same spirit which characterizes an earlier age."

Herbert Spencer, in his essay on " Justice," says that he once favored woman suffrage " from the point of view of a general principle of individual rights." Later he finds that this cannot be maintained, because he " discovers mental and emotional differences between the sexes which disqualify women from the burden of government and the exercise of its functions." He also considers it absurd for women to claim the vote and military exemption in the name of equality.

Science has told us of the active, as well as the passive, part that the mother plays in the growth of the embryo, and at the same time has told us that the sex of that embryo is determined by the nourishing power of the mother. The commonplace statistics of the census come in with their verifying word, and we find that in rude times and hard conditions more boys are born. Gentle conditions and abundance are favorable to the birth of girls. Here is the same story we have learned so often. Man the protector, woman the protected. Woman the inspiring force, man the organizing and physical power.

So the Bible, Science, and Republican government, according to Suffragist and Anti-suffragist, have planted themselves squarely on the sex issue. It is solid standing-ground, and neither apparent irrelevancy nor real antagonism will dislodge the argument.

Dr. Jacobi, in her address before the Constitutional Convention, said : " Still, all women do not demand the suffrage. We are sometimes told that the thousands of women who do want the suffrage must wait until those who are now indifferent, or even hostile, can be converted from their position. Gentlemen, we declare that theory is preposterous. It is true that the exercise of an independent sovereignty necessitates the demonstration of a very considerable amount of independence. A rebel state that cannot break its own blockade may not call upon a foreign power to move from its neutrality to do so. But the demand for equal suffrage is in nowise analogous to a claim for independent sovereignty. It is rather analogous to the claim to the protection of existing laws, which any group of people, or even a single person, may make."

Under a democratic government a claim for equal suffrage is a claim to share the independent sovereignty that protects, and therefore it cannot be analogous to a claim for protection, individual or otherwise, under that sovereignty. Does Dr. Jacobi mean that in asking for suffrage she does not ask to be as much an independent sovereign as any masculine voter of them all ? The comparison of woman's claims to suffrage to the pro-

tection afforded by existing laws, suggests a nar-
rowing of the demand to fit the requirements of
an apparently hopeless struggle for a majority
vote of women.

The Government is spoken of by Suffragists as
if it were something exterior to and apart from
the individual voters—a code of laws that had
been set going and would run of itself, the laws
being changed by more or fewer votes, but the
power to execute being automatic and continuous.
As this is the opposite of the actual situation,
these rebels will have to " break their own blockade " like any others.

The " pacific blocade " that is enforced by the
Quaker guns of this movement has its peaceful
war-cries.   One of the most exultant is an allusion
to the expression " We the people " in the preamble of our national Constitution, with the question whether " people " does not include women.
A reading of the entire preamble shows that, of
the six achievements there specified as the purpose of the Constitution, every one is a thing that
only men can do—with the possible exception of
the fifth, which proposes rather vaguely to " promote the general welfare."

As to the thousands of women who want the
vote, there are some figures as to the majority that
" are indifferent or even hostile." I see by the
pamphlet published by the New York State Suffrage Association, that they have but 1,600 paying members, which is not one in a thousand of

the women in the State over twenty years of age. As Mrs. Winslow Crannell has made a careful computation from figures published in the "Woman's Journal," edited by Henry B. Blackwell and his daughter Alice Stone Blackwell, I quote her results: In Maine there are but 12 Suffragists to every 100,000 of the people; in New Hampshire, but 5 to every 100,000; in Massachusetts, but 51 to every 100,000; in Connecticut, but 23 to every 100,000. Pennsylvania has but 14 in 100,000; Kentucky has 32 to 100,000; Michigan, but 6 to 100,000; Illinois has 13 to 100,000; Ohio has 11 to 100,000; Iowa has 6 to 100,000; Virginia, but 1 to 100,000; New Jersey, 8 to 100,000; Arkansas, 3 to 100,000; South Carolina, 3 to 100,000. Calfornia has 33 in every 100,000, and Maryland has 6 in 100,000. If the suffrage is claimed for tax-paying women, it can be shown that there are, in New York State, for instance, at least 1,500,000 women who do not pay taxes. But, as a matter of fact, the tax-paying women of this State were among the first signers of Anti-suffrage petitions.

# CHAPTER XI.

THE tenth count in the Suffrage Declaration is : " He has usurped the prerogative of Jehovah himself, claiming it as his right to assign for her a sphere of action, when that belongs to her conscience and to her God."

In the " History of Woman Suffrage," the editors say : " Quite as many false ideas prevail as to woman's true position in the home as elsewhere. Womanhood is the great fact of her life ; wifehood and motherhood are but incidental relations."

The first legislation demanded by the Suffragists was that which called for a change of the marriage laws, so as to admit of divorce, first for drunkenness, and later for several other causes. In discussing the matter in convention, Mrs. Stanton presented resolutions that declared, among other things, " That any constitution, compact, or covenant between human beings that failed to produce or promote human happiness, could not, in the nature of things, be of any force or authority ; and it would be not only a right, but a duty, to abolish it. That though marriage

302

be in itself divinely founded, and is fortified as
an institution by innumerable analogies in the
whole kingdom of universal nature, still a true marriage is only known by its results; and like the
fountain, if pure, will reveal only pure manifesta-
tions. That observation and experience daily
show how incompetent are men, as individuals, or
as governments, to select partners in business,
teachers for their children, ministers of their religion, or makers, adjudicators or administrators of
their laws; and as the same weakness and blind-
ness must attend in the selection of matrimonial
partners, the dictates of humanity and common-
sense alike show that the latter and most important contract should no more be perpetual than
either or all of the former."

In supporting these resolutions, Mrs. Stanton
said, "I place man above all governments, ecclesiastical and civil—all constitutions and laws."
"In the settlement of any question, we must
simply consider the highest good of the individual." Antoinette Brown Blackwell followed Mrs.
Stanton with a series of resolutions in which
she opposed her, and defended the sanctity of
marriage. Wendell Phillips moved that neither
series of resolutions be entered on the journal.
Mr. Garrison said they did not come together to
settle the question of marriage, but he should be
sorry to rule out Mrs. Stanton's resolutions and
speeches. Miss Anthony said: "I hope Mr.
Phillips will withdraw his motion. . . . I totally

dissent from the idea that this question does not belong on this platform. Marriage has ever been a one-sided matter. By it, man gains all, woman loses all. Tyrant law and lust reign supreme with him ; meek submission and ready obedience alone befit her. . . . By law, public sentiment, and religion, from the time of Moses down to the present day, woman has never been thought of other than as a piece of property, to be disposed of at the will and pleasure of man. . . . She must accept marriage as man proffers it, or not at all."

The resolutions were carried and recorded, and are published to this day, with added testimony to the same effect from a hundred Suffrage sources. We turn back to trace one of the lines through which this teaching has come down. The Suffrage leaders mention as special inspirers of their movement besides Ernestine Rose (who seconded Mrs. Stanton's resolutions) and Frances Wright, Margaret Fuller and Mary Wollstonecraft. In the writings of those women we find the same sentiments set forth with delicacy or vulgarity, according to the nature of the writer. Margaret Fuller, in her Dial essay, published in 1843, "The Great Lawsuit — Man Versus Woman, Woman Versus Man," says : " It is the fault of marriage, and of the present relation between the sexes, that the woman belongs to the man, instead of forming a whole with him. It is a vulgar error to suppose that love—a love—is to woman her whole existence. She is also born for Truth and

Love in their universal energy. Would she but assume her inheritance, Mary would not be the only virgin mother." Mary Wollstonecraft believed that marriage consisted solely of mutual affection, and that there should be no outward promise or tie to bind. If love were to die, the heart should seek other affinity. The licentious words of Frances Wright need not be repeated. With Mephistophelian promptings, Ernestine Rose stood forever a-tip-toe, whispering in the ear of the purer American feeling that would often have faltered. At the time of the passing of Mrs. Stanton's resolutions she said: "But what is marriage? A human institution, called out by the needs of the social, affectional human nature for human purposes. . . . If it is demonstrated that the real objects are frustrated, I ask, in the name of individual happiness and social morality and well-being, why should such a marriage be binding for life? . . . I ask that personal cruelty to the wife may be made a State's-prison offence, for which divorce shall be granted. Wilful desertion for one year should be a sufficient cause for divorce. . . . Habitual intemperance, or any other vice which makes the husband or wife intolerable and abhorrent to the other, ought to be sufficient cause for divorce." Essentially the same idea was repeated by Dr. Hulda Gunn in a recent Suffrage meeting.

In asking for laws that carried out these claims, or some of them, Mrs. Stanton said, in addressing

20

the New York Legislature in 1854 : "If you take the highest view of marriage as a Divine relation, which love alone can constitute and sanctify, then of course human legislation can only recognize it. . . . But if you regard marriage as a civil contract, then let it be subject to the same laws that control all other contracts.   Do not make it a kind of half-human, half-divine institution, which you may build up but cannot regulate."

These doctrines—from those of Frances Wright to those of Mrs. Stanton and Miss Anthony—were put forth in the name of social purity and true marriage.. A great body of Suffragists never have accepted them.   They were repugnant, in this form, to a majority who were demanding "equal rights."   In January, 1871, Mr. Hooker (husband of Isabella Beecher Hooker), said in the New York Evening Post : "The persons who advocate easy divorce would advocate it just as strongly if there was no Suffrage movement. The two have no necessary connection.   Indeed, one of the strongest arguments in favor of Woman Suffrage is, that the marriage relation will be safer with women to vote and legislate upon it than where the voting and legislation are left wholly to men.   Women will always be wives and mothers, above all things else.   This law of nature cannot be changed, and I know of nobody who desires to change it."   As he had just been referring to "persons who advocated easy divorce," and who originated the Suffrage movement, his statement that he knew of nobody who desired to change marriage seems funny.

It was one of the matters remarked upon with satisfaction by Suffrage leaders during our Constitutional Convention Suffrage campaign, that such a large number of speakers advocated Suffrage because of its advantage to the home. Mrs. Cora Seabury said : " Where woman is, homes naturally exist, and not without her. The 'divine veracity in nature,' which in her case has survived the chaos of ages and the varying civil:zation of six thousand years, is not now to be disproved by an incident comparatively so trivial as that of taking the ballot." Dr. Jacobi puts the idea in this way : " Mr. Goldwin Smith declares that woman suffrage aims at such a ' sexual revolution' as must cause the ' dissolution of the family.' The Suffrage claim does not aim at this ; it seeks only to formulate, recognize, and define the revolution already effected, yet which leaves the family intact. The *Patria Potestas* is gone. A man has lost, first, the right to kill his own son, then the right to order the marriage of his daughter, then the right to absorb the property of his wife. Nevertheless, he survives, and the family, shorn of its portentous rights, bids fair in America to remain the happiest of all conceivable natural institutions ; more profound than society, so immeasurably deeper than politics that the fortunate wife, daughter, or sister is puzzled when the two are mentioned in the same breath."

All these writers agree in demanding the ballot in order to make some essential change in woman's condition. Some of them hold that this change cannot be made unless the relations of wife and mother can be set aside when the individual considers them detrimental; others hold that it can be made and leave the relations intact; and one believes that this change is already so far made, while the relations are still intact, that nothing need be feared from further change. It reduces itself to matter of opinion and prophecy on the part of those who agree with the early leaders that essential change is needed, but do not agree with them as to the steps necessary. The appeal must be to facts.

The originators of the movement ought to know what the movement meant. The marriage laws were the first attacked, and are still being hammered at in favor of divorce, although legislation has outrun their demand in changing the outgrown laws in regard to property and contracts. Mr. Hooker said: " The persons who advocate easy divorce would advocate it just as strongly if there was no Suffrage movement." How can that be, when the women who inspired the Suffrage movement, and who began it and still carry it on, proclaimed this as a necessary part? But, this question aside, it may be said that the marriage relation has been the most unsafe in the hands of the women whose idea of equality either repudiates it outright or inveighs

against its present status. From the revolutionary and infidel portion of France, from which it
sprang, to the recently dead Oneida Community,
who but women who imbibed the doctrine that
marriage was bondage, have sustained the various
forms of license which called itself freedom?
Transcendentalism and Libertinism worked together, and both found women who could be
fitted to the task of destroying the home.

Mrs. Seabury avers that where woman is, homes
will naturally exist. Homes have not existed
"naturally." There was a long, long time in
human history when not a dream of a home existed. From lawless individualism to tribal life,
from tribe to clan, from the clan, at last, through
mighty struggles, the family was evolved—the
final grouping of the race—the social unit. That
point was not reached until man the savage, man
the rover, had consented to be bound, and bound
for life, to one woman. It has been one object
of Christian civilization to hold man to this saving compact. First to hold his spirit by affection
for wife and child, and next to hold his material
interests for the sake of society. The work has so
well progressed that to-day the man's family is
dearer to him than his own life. He will live for
them, and fight for them; and the women who
proclaim that man is woman's enemy, are the
assassins of their own peace and of the growing
peace of home.

A proof that "women will not always be wives

and mothers above all things else," is to be found in the story of the women who have engaged in intrigue from the days of ancient Egppt. A woman State senator-elect says: "I am a Mormon, and believe in polygamy." The organizations that are first to proclaim the so-called freedom of woman from the marriage bond, are the same that would repudiate all government, human and divine.

But man has no more set the bounds of woman's life than woman has set those of man's. It is false to say that man has "usurped the prerogative of Jehovah," in assigning her a sphere of action. He has assigned neither her sphere nor his own. Their spheres have been worked out from the conditions that made them male and female. The ideal that faith could picture was presented in the Old Testament, and when Christ said, "For the hardness of your hearts Moses commanded to write a bill of divorcement, but in the beginning it was not so," he spoke the ultimate word. Save for adultery, the family was not to be broken, and the laws of modern life, which grow freer in every other respect, are approaching nearer to this model as society progresses, and most rapidly so in the most progressive states.

There is a fine bit of unconscious humor in Miss Anthony's remark that "Woman must accept marriage as man proffers it, or not at all." Man is at present blinded by the belief that he must proffer marriage as woman will accept it, or not at all. Society has lodged with her what Mrs. Stanton calls "only the veto power." Miss Anthony and Mrs. Stanton apparently wish the women to do the proffering, the accepting, and the rejecting. With so insignificant a part assigned him, it would seem a pity that there should be a sort of necessity for man to play in the marriage rôle at all. When Suffrage leaders have so arranged matters that the bride retains her maiden name, she can spend her summers in Europe and her winters in Florida, while her husband works all the year round in New York to support her, without her being subjected to the mortification of seeming to desert the man whose name she bears.

You cannot teach this untruth to the girl without teaching it to the boy. The struggle of civilization has been to teach that manhood was not the great fact of man's life, and he has learned it through the chivalry and tenderness that appealed to and developed his higher nature. But if once he understands that woman does not hold herself in need of his chivalry and tenderness, the husbandhood and fatherhood that now bind him to one sacred vow of married love, and tame the savage within him, will not long prevent him from seeing his own advantage in the new order.

Wifehood and motherhood 'incidental relations.' They are incidental! Incidental not only to the continuance of the race in civilization, but to all that is best and holiest in that continuance. The

mothers of the Rebellion say : " The love of offspring, common to all orders of women and all
forms of animal life, tender and beautiful as it is,
cannot as a sentiment rank with conjugal love.
The one calls out only the negative virtues that
belong to the apathetic classes, such as patience,
endurance, self-sacrifice, exhausting the brain
forces, ever giving, asking nothing in return ; the
other, the outgrowth of the two supreme powers
in nature, the positive and negative magnetism,
the centrifugal and centripetal forces, the masculine and feminine elements, possessing the divine
power of creation in the universe of thought and
action. Two pure souls fused into one by an impassioned love. This is marriage, and this is the
only corner-stone of an enduring home."

The " homes " built solely upon this corner-
stone have not endured in this country. The
children born under such principles are taken care
of by the " Community " in a building apart from
that occupied by the " pure souls." The " institutional " bringing up of children was lately advocated in this city by Mrs. Stanton Blatch at Suffrage meetings.

The virtues that the Suffrage leaders denounce
as " apathetic " are those that Christ signalized as
the heavenly virtues, and are those which heroes
emulate, whether they be women or men.

Dr. Jacobi says the Suffrage movement, " aims
only to regulate and define the revolution already
effected, and which leaves the family intact." **I**

think it has been proven from words and acts that it does aim at just such a " sexual revolution " as threatens the family with dissolution. It aimed to accomplish this by every means in its power, by an industrialism which it desired should make woman independent of man, by divorce laws, and by the use of the ballot. Who has shorn man of all his portentous rights? Man himself, through the influence of woman. Is it likely, then, that he was taking steps in the direction of the destruction of his own home? He was endeavoring to build it on those sure foundations that make it what it is. He can build if woman occupies, but he cannot both fight for the home and against it. Circumstances, and not Suffrage cries, have forced or enticed woman into the trades and professions. She has gone farther afield for her work, partly because the Ægis of home is more broadly spread than it formerly could be on account of the very strength of the marriage tie, which makes honor, home, and woman more secure. So far as she has gone to help the home, and because of love of it, such causes have not hurt the family life, and will not. But when we come to Suffrage we have met a different matter. The vote is not an affair of feeling or opinion, like religious belief. The fact that the men of the family are the natural defenders of law, and the women are not, is seen at close quarters in the home, and in case of opposite votes and any serious resulting action, the father and son must stand in the attitude of actual physical as well as political antagonism to the mother and daughter. If it came to an issue, man would have to decide whether he would defend his own opinion, expressed in his ballot, or the opposite opinion expressed by his wife in her ballot. And the mere suggestion of difference in family opinion, final action upon which could only be taken by a resort to that in which the men must always be superior, would not only endanger family life and peace, but would develop a fatal inequality between the sexes. If the women of the family vote with the men, they only double the vote and the expense, without changing the result; if they vote against the men, they stand in the ridiculous attitude of opposing them where they cannot do more than pull hair, or inviting a revolution which they cannot stay.

As to the possibility of this, there are a few striking and suggestive facts at hand. The sound judgment and law-abiding element of this country expressed itself in no uncertain tones at the late election. After the defeat of Mr. Bryan, he was given a tremendous demonstration of approval at Denver, in which the women played a conspicuous part. Mrs. Bradford said: "The women tried to welcome you to the White House. When a few more stars have been added to the Equal Suffrage banner, the women *will* welcome you to the White House." Mrs. Patterson, President of the Equal Suffrage League, said in seconding the address of welcome: "Women of Colorado, I present to you the first president of the twentieth century—William Jennings Bryan." An invalid of whom I know, travelled from California to her home in Colorado in order to cast her vote for Bryan, while her husband cast his for McKinley in California. Mrs. Cannon, of Utah, was elected on the Free-Silver ticket, against her husband on the Gold-Standard ticket. Mrs. Cronine, a Populist member of the legislature of Colorado, is reported as saying: "It hurt my husband, a life-long Republican, to see me vote against his party and carry both our children with me." Should there be political disturbance in Colorado and Utah, in 1900, here are three husbands on record who might be called upon by the United States authorities to put down by force, perhaps to kill, those whose lawlessness their wives had instigated and abetted. In one instance the man's own sons may fight against him, impelled to do so by the lessons taught by their mother. It requires no stretch of fancy to see the possibility of civil war brought to the doors of every home, when women vote. And the occasion that would bring it would not be the saving of the Nation's life, but its overthrow; not freedom for an oppressed class, but mingled bondage and license for a sex now free; not the preservation of home, but its destruction. The Suffrage women who here among us are talking so foolishly about arbitration and universal peace, seem to have no conception that with their next breath they are endeavoring to establish the conditions for the most horrible of conflicts—that of Sex. So far from the " taking of the ballot " being " trivial," it is the most serious and dangerous business in which a woman can engage.

The home is not a natural institution unless it is maintained by natural means, and woman suffrage and the home are incompatible. John Bright, in reply to Mr. Theodore Stanton's question why he opposed suffrage, said, "I cannot give you all the reasons for the view I take, but I act from the belief that to introduce women into the strife of political life would be a great evil to them, and that to our own sex no possible good could arise. When women are not safe under the charge or care of fathers, husbands, brothers, and sons, it is the fault of our non-civilization, and not of our laws. As civilization founded on Christian principles advances, women will gain all that is right for them to have, though they are not seen contending in the strife of political parties. In my experience I have observed evil results to many women who have entered hotly into political conflict and discussion. I would save them from it."

How true this is, and how wise are the fears expressed by Mr. Bright, we realize afresh at every study of the exciting campaign of November, 1896. The Woman's Journal, the Suffrage organ, published a letter from its California correspondent descriptive of the work of their women in watching the count on the Suffrage amendment. One woman who felt "terribly blue" says that a man patted her on the shoulder and told her to keep up her courage, and she says : " It broke me up, I can tell you, for I never could stand sympathy. If people will let me alone, I can grit my teeth and stand it, but when they say kind things to me I go to pieces. However, as I was bound I would not show those men how badly I felt, and give them a chance to say women were hysterical, I smiled weakly—very weakly, I'm afraid—but still it was a smile and passed as such. Then I began to get sick—ye gods! how sick! The excitement in the booth stopped, but there was an excitement in my head that had not been there before! Everything got black and began to go round. They could have counted us out a dozen times, and I should never have known the difference." Again the correspondent says : " Mrs. W. was so tired that she broke down." " Mrs. Babcock waxed eloquent, and had the meeting in tears. Miss Shaw said she wanted to speak of one who had been forgotten, because she came here before any of the rest, and worked so hard that she had ruined her health, and lay pale and white on her couch at home. She stood there, and the tears rolled down her cheeks, and she didn't try to wipe them away. Every one was crying. Mrs. Blinn said, ' I cannot speak. I feel too much to say anything,' and then she broke down and

cried. Mrs. McCann soon had everybody crying
about Miss Hay, and when Miss Hay got up she
was crying too. So we had a very weepy morning, you see." In describing the departure of
Miss Anthony and Rev. Anna Shaw for the East
she says : " Oh, it was awful ! awful ! The whole
thing was like a funeral."

With the steady improvement in machinery and
in education, the wife and mother can be more
and more relieved of work. But the home
depends as much as ever upon her love, her skill,
her care. She now has means, which science has
just taught the world, of learning how to provide,
on proper principles, for children, how to dress
sensibly, cook wholesomely, make the home sanitary. Nursing is a fine art now, and comforts
can be placed within the reach of every invalid, if
the mother knows how to do it. If home is to
be hospitable, and a centre of social influence, all
the artistic and homely powers are demanded. If
the family is to be well-dressed, the mother must
attend to it. If home is to be beautiful, the
mother and daughter must make it so. In these
days, there is little need of slaving ; and there is
a glimpse ahead of leisure for thought and self-
culture such as men would find it hard to make.
The long and enforced retirement of maternity
may prove a time for most valuable improvement.
In our social life there is too little culture that is
the result of absorption by a quiet process of
mental assimilation. The place where this can be

best achieved is in the home. The danger of our fascinating modern life, with its endless calls and opportunities outside, lies in the strain it puts upon systems that are far more delicately organized than man's. Nature meant that women should have periods of quiet. Let us honor our own natures, exalt our own opportunities, love and lead our own lives, and so bless the world and the Republic through perfected homes.

I have considered this question mainly from the view-point of the wife and mother ; but the home relations are vastly broader. In regard to their whole scope, some of the Suffrage leaders have uttered this dictum : " The isolated household is responsible for a large share of woman's ignorance and degradation." If this declaration does not mean that the Suffrage movement aims to tear down the individual home, it means nothing. The world must judge which system is responsible for the larger share of woman's ignorance and degradation.

# CHAPTER XII.

In the opening of this volume I have given it as my opinion that the movement to obtain the elective franchise for woman is not in harmony with those through which woman and government have made progress. I have spoken of the marvellous forward impulse that has marked the passage of the last half-century, and have mentioned the growth of religious liberty, the founding of foreign and home missions, the extinction of slavery, the temperance movement, the settlement of the West, the opening of the professions and trades to women, the progress of mechanical invention, the sudden advance of science, the civil war, and the natural play of free conditions, as among the causes of this impulse. I have pointed out the fact that the Suffrage movement has nearly reached its semi-centennial year, and has made a record by which its relation to these progressive forces can be judged, and I have appealed from the repetition of its claims to the verdict of its accomplishment.

In the second chapter I have considered the

320

growth of republican forms the world over, and endeavored to show that the dogma of Woman Suffrage is fundamentally at war with true democratic principles, and that, practically, woman suffrage has been allied with despotism, monarchy, and ecclesiastical oppression on the one hand, and with the powers of license and misrule that assail republican government on the other.

In the third chapter I attempt to prove this further by a study of the origin of the Suffrage movement, and by its relation to the Government of the United States. I try to refute the two propositions which it has put forth as solid resting-ground for woman's claim to the elective franchise in this land—"Taxation without representation is tyranny," and "There is no just government without the consent of the governed." I have also set forth the difference between municipal and constitutional suffrage, and shown that the extension of school suffrage, so far from being a stepping-stone to full suffrage, affords another evidence that such full suffrage is unprogressive and undemocratic. It is held that regulated, universal manhood suffrage is the natural and only safe basis of government.

In the fourth chapter I consider the early relation of the Suffrage movement to the causes of anti-slavery and temperance. I also discuss the attitude of the Suffrage leaders during the civil

21

war, and indicate that the Suffrage movement
was not patriotic, and was a hindrance to emancipation and reform.

The fifth chapter treats of the connection of the
Suffrage movement with the change that has
taken place in the laws, and it contains a synopsis
of the present laws of New York regarding
women.   From this study it appears that the Suffrage movement did not originate the change in
the laws; that many changes most vigorously
urged by its associations never have been enacted; and that change of laws has not been so
much sought as a voice upon change of laws—
the fact being, that the vote *per se* has been
urged as the panacea for all woman's wrongs.

The sixth chapter deals with Woman Suffrage
and the trades.   It shows that this movement was
not instrumental in opening the trades to women;
that the conditions of industrial life are not
changed in such essentials as would involve a
change of sex relation to Government; and that,
so far from altering the basis of government,
industrialism has introduced new problems of
such grave import that security in the enforcement of law is doubly necessary. . It shows, furthermore, that socialistic labor has been naturally
the friend of Woman Suffrage, while the safer
and sounder organizations have extended sympa-
thetic help to woman.

The seventh chapter discusses the connection of Woman Suffrage with the professions. It aims to show that here, too, suffrage has not been necessary to gain, for women who were fitted to hold it, an honorable place; and, in regard to the places they have not yet entered, it is held that the impulse must come from within. It is argued that, in the professions, as in the trades, Suffrage effort has hindered more than it has helped, and that in the West its practical working is the most damaging thing that has attended woman's real progress.

The eighth chapter considers the connection of Woman Suffrage with education. Its conclusions are, that not education, but coeducation, was the persistent demand of Suffragists, and that woman's advancement in college and university was wrought out by the impulse gained from women who opposed the Suffrage idea, and made practical by men to whom also that idea was repugnant. It is suggested that women who could prepare and defend the ignorant Suffrage Woman's Bible have no right to utter a syllable in protest of the educational ideas of men and women who are competent to speak on the subject, and whose verdict has been, on the whole, for separate study during collegiate age, wherever such could be afforded, while it is not disputed that coeducation has its place and its uses.

324 *OMAN AND THE REPUBLIC.*

The ninth chapter presents Woman Suffrage in its relation to the church. It first discusses, briefly, a few points in the Suffrage Woman's Bible, published in New York in 1895. This is a commentary on such passages in the Pentateuch as relate to women, and the title "Rev." is prefixed to four names of editors on its title-page. This book, or rather a book of which this is the first instalment, was promised by Suffrage writers and speakers from the beginning. It is considered to contain the consummate blossom of the mind that first expounded the Suffrage theory—the mind that grasped it as a whole, in its full meaning and intent, and never has wavered in expression as to its ultimate object and the means by which that object is to be sought. This chapter sets forth, in few words, the present writer's view of woman in the creation, and of St. Paul's attitude toward woman. The chapter further discusses woman's early preaching in this country, and shows that it has not been such as to build up religion or the state, but has been such as to suggest that, while the possibilities of her nature tend to make her supreme in capacity to point the way to higher regions, it also contains qualities that may render her peculiarly dangerous as a public leader.

The tenth chapter, entitled "Woman Suffrage and Sex," alludes briefly to the social evil, and then discusses the Suffrage ideas in regard to sex as explained by both their older and more recent writers. It discusses the disabilities of sex in relation to the suffrage—the difficulties in the way of jury duty, police duty, and office-holding —and draws the conclusion that the fulfilment of such necessary work of the voting citizen is practically an impossibility for woman, and has been found to be so in the Western States.

The eleventh chapter has for its title " Woman Suffrage and the Home." It sets forth the belief that the Suffrage movement strikes a blow squarely at the home and the marriage relation, and that the ballot is demanded by its most representative leaders for the purpose of making woman independent of the present social order. It argues that communism is the natural ally of Suffrage, and that, as homes did not spring out of the ground, they will not remain where men and women alter the mutual relations out of which the institution of home has slowly grown.

The general conclusion of the book is, that woman's relation to the Republic is as important as man's. Woman deals with the beginnings of life; man, with the product made from those beginnings; and this fact marks the difference in their spheres, and reveals woman's immense advantage in moral opportunity. It also suggests the incalculable loss in case her work is not done or ill done. In a ruder age the evident value of power that could deal with developed force was most appreciated; but such is not now the case. It lies with us to prove that education, instead of causing us to attempt work that belongs even less to the cultivated woman than to the ignorant, is fitting us to train up statesmen who will be the first to do us honor. The American Republic depends finally for its existence and its greatness upon the virtue and ability of American womanhood. If our ideals are mistaken or unworthy, then there will be ultimately no republic for men to govern or defend. When women are Buddhists, the men build up an empire of India. When women are Mohammedans, the men construct an Empire of Turkey. When women are Christians, men can conceive and bring into being a Republic like the United States. Woman is to implant the faith, man is to cause the Nation's faith to show itself in works. More and more these duties overlap, but they cannot become interchangeable while sex continues to divide the race into the two halves of what should become a perfect whole. Woman Suffrage aims to sweep away this natural distinction, and make humanity a mass of individuals with an indiscriminate sphere. The attack is now bold and now subtle, now malicious and now mistaken; but it is at all times an attack. The greatest danger with which this land is threatened comes from the ignorant and persistent zeal of some of its women. They abuse the freedom under which they live, and to gain an impossible power would fain destroy the Government that alone can protect them. The majority of women have no sympathy with this movement; and in their enlightenment, and in the consistent wisdom of our men, lies our hope of defeating this unpatriotic, unintelligent, and unjustifiable assault upon the integrity of the American Republic.

New York, *March, 1897.*

THE END.

www.ingramcontent.com/pod-product-compliance
Lightning Source LLC
Chambersburg PA
CBHW021211270326
41929CB00010B/1082